ISBN 978-1-331-31725-8
PIBN 10173469

English
Français
Deutsche
Italiano
Español
Português

www.forgottenbooks.com

Mythology Photography **Fiction**
Fishing Christianity **Art** Cooking
Essays Buddhism Freemasonry
Medicine **Biology** Music **Ancient**
Egypt Evolution Carpentry Physics
Dance Geology **Mathematics** Fitness
Shakespeare **Folklore** Yoga Marketing
Confidence Immortality Biographies
Poetry **Psychology** Witchcraft
Electronics Chemistry History **Law**
Accounting **Philosophy** Anthropology
Alchemy Drama Quantum Mechanics
Atheism Sexual Health **Ancient History**
Entrepreneurship Languages Sport
Paleontology Needlework Islam
Metaphysics Investment Archaeology
Parenting Statistics Criminology
Motivational

ENTRANCE INTO THE KINGDOM

OR

Reward According to Works

BY

R. GOVETT, M.A.

(Sometime Fellow of Worcester College, Oxford)

PART I

SECOND EDITION

LONDON

CHARLES J. THYNNE

WHITEFRIARS ST., E.C.4

OCT., 1922

PRINTED IN GREAT BRITAIN BY THE DEVONSHIRE PRESS, TORQUAY.

PREFACE

FAITH, connecting the sinner with the perfect work of Christ, brings present acceptance before God, and eternal life as its blessed issue. The works of man, whether converted or unconverted, avail not to obtain the pardon of sins, or everlasting bliss. God is a Sovereign, as is shown in his electing whom he will, sustaining their faith through a world of dangers, and glorifying them at last.

These truths were established at the Reformation, on the sure foundation of Scripture. Good works, it was seen, are the proofs of a living faith, and they are the true fruits of it. But this leaves untouched the further inquiry—WHAT ARE THE EFFECTS OF GOOD OR EVIL WORKS ON THE FUTURE POSITION OF ONE ALREADY JUSTIFIED ? The ensuing pages open the enquiry to some extent ; and they do so, in the only safe manner, by a consideration of some portions of Holy Writ which speak of these things.

1. The Scriptures affirm that all believers shall give account at the judgment seat of Christ : Rom. xiv., 10—12 ; 2 Cor., v. 9, 10 ; Heb. x., 30.

2. They declare that the principle of judgment shall be according to works. That is, regard will be had both to the nature of the works, and to their degree of good or evil : Matt. xvi, 24—27 ; Rev. ii., 23 ; xxii, 12.

Does not, then, the New Testament suppose that believers are agents producing both good and evil works ? Does it not anticipate that some would be guilty of sloth, or be found wanting in good works ? *What then shall be the issue of such investigation ?*

Can any inquiry be more important to the saint ?

The merits of Christ are the answer to the demands of the law of God upon us, as responsible moral creatures who have broken his law. They free Christians from eternal death ; they open to them eternal life. But the point to be considered is : Whether the Saviour and his apostles do not speak of an account to be rendered to Christ by his believing *servants ;* when both their offences against *professed servitude,* and their actions in obedience to his claims will come before him ?

The faith of Christians in general, as it appears to the author, embraces and enjoys *present rest* in God, through the work of Christ. But it has overlooked the doctrine of the *future rest* of the kingdom as the reward for present exertion. Now faith in the kingdom will alone produce works meet for the kingdom.

The history of David's mighty men, arranged in his kingdom according to their acts of bravery during the time of his rejection, is given as the principle to be applied to us. *Twice* is the record given ; so important did the Holy Spirit consider it : 2 Sam. xxiii ; 1 Chron. xi.

It is not expected that these truths will ever be popular. They boast no great names ; they flatter not. They rest only on the proofs of God's word. They have to contend with the remains of evil adhering even to the saint. It is a novelty too ; though old on the page of Scripture. The Christianity of the present age is much relaxing : the influences of the world are creeping on it and benumbing it. Do not Christians love to hear only of God's mercy, and of their privileges ? But we must also speak of the demands of the God of equity upon those gifted with privileges.

The doctrine here propounded stands on the passages adduced : though these are not all in which it is affirmed. The second Epistle of Peter, though not here touched on, is very full to the point. " In the mouth of two or three witnesses every word shall be established," is the declaration of God. Here are more than twice three ; and the reader may soon find others for himself. Should any desire to impugn these views ; they must show that the passages adduced do not contain the doctrines supposed. If reward according to the believer's works be taught in these and other Scriptures, objections drawn from other doctrines, or from the difficulty of reconciling the present text with seemingly conflicting testimonies of Holy Writ, will not be accounted sufficient. Does the Holy Ghost any where teach that loss will be inflicted on the believer for his evil works ? Does he affirm, that reward in the kingdom is to be given to the believer in proportion to his works ? If so, that is enough. The doctrine is established, all objections to the contrary notwithstanding.

In order that no mistake may arise, let it be clearly observed, that THE DOCTRINE OF REWARD FOR GOOD WORKS APPLIES ONLY TO THOSE JUSTIFIED ALREADY. Then the truth is amply guarded against being misapplied by the ungodly as the way to justification. The doctrine of reward according to works does indeed affect the wicked also. Each act of trespass on their part is increasing their damnation. But that is not treated of here.

Norwich, June 21st, 1853.

To the remarkable contrasts between the Epistles to the Romans and to the Hebrews, the author desires to add one which was overlooked.

Both Epistles treat of FAITH. Romans exhibits it as the source of justification without works. But Hebrews presents it as the fruitful parent of all holy deeds.

CONTENTS

CHAPTER I

ETERNAL LIFE A GIFT:

THE

KINGDOM OF CHRIST A REWARD

THE propositions intended to be proved in the present pages are two.

1. THAT ETERNAL LIFE IS GOD'S UNCONDITIONAL GIFT TO BELIEVERS.

2. THAT BELIEVERS' PARTICIPATION IN THE KINGDOM OF CHRIST IS CONDITIONAL ON THEIR CONDUCT, AS GOOD OR EVIL.

To the Jew under the law it was proposed of God to win eternal life by his own obedience to the divine commands. This is proved by the following passages :

1. " And behold one came and said unto him, Good Master, (teacher) *what good thing shall I do, that I may have eternal life ?* And he said unto him, why callest thou me good ? There is none good but one, that is God ; *but if thou wishest to* enter into life, keep the commandments.* He saith unto him, Which ? Jesus said, Thou shalt do no murder, thou shalt not commit adultery, thou shalt not steal, thou shalt not bear false witness, honour thy father and thy mother : and, thou shalt love thy neighbour as thyself : " Matt. xix, 16—19. So Mark x, 17 ; Luke xviii, 18.

2. " And behold a certain lawyer stood up, and tempted him, saying, *Master, what shall I do to inherit eternal life ?* He said unto him, *What is written in the law ?* how readest thou ? And he answering said, Thou shalt love the Lord thy God with all

* Θελεις εισελθειν.

thy heart, and with all thy soul, and with all thy strength, and with all thy mind ; and thy neighbour as thyself. And he said unto him, Thou hast answered right ; *this do and thou shalt live :* " Luke x, 25—28.

But these righteous conditions have never been fulfilled by any son of man, save Jesus. The new ground therefore taken by the Gospel, is, that eternal life is granted at once to the Christian by faith in the work of Messiah, as the ensuing declarations prove.

1. " This is the record (testimony) that *God hath given to us eternal life, and this life is in his Son.* He that hath the Son hath life, and he that hath not the Son of God hath not life : " I John v. 11, 12.

2. " My sheep hear my voice, and I know them, and they follow me. *And I give unto them eternal life, and they shall never perish, neither shall any pluck them out of my hand :* " John x, 27, 28.

3. " As thou hast given him (thy Son) power over all flesh, *that he should give eternal life to as many as thou hast given him :* " John xvii, 2.

Eternal life is attached to faith in the revelation of the new name of God under the Gospel ; or, as it is sometimes described, it is granted to those who believe on the name of the Son of God.

4. " As Moses lifted up the serpent in the wilderness, so must the Son of man be lifted up, *that whosoever believeth in him should not perish but have eternal life.* For God so loved the world, that *he gave his only begotten Son, that whosoever believeth on him should not perish but have everlasting life :* " John iii, 14—16.

5. " *He that believeth on the Son hath everlasting life :* and he that believeth not the Son shall not see life, but the wrath of God abideth on him : " John iii, 36.

6. " And this is the will of him that sent me, that every *one which seeth the Son and believeth on him may have everlasting life,* and I will raise him up at the last day : " John vi, 40.

7. " *Verily I say unto you, he that believeth on me hath everlasting life* · " John vi, 47.

Confirmatory declarations may be found in John v, 24 ; xvii, 3 ; 1 Tim. i, 16 ; 1 John v, 13, 20.

I now pass on to the second proposition.

THE PARTICIPATION OF BELIEVERS IN THE KINGDOM OF
GOD DEPENDS UPON THEIR CONDUCT AFTER THEY BEGIN
TO BELIEVE.

And first we inquire, what is meant by " the kingdom
of God ? "

Most take it to signify the gospel dispensation—the
spiritual reign of grace.

I suppose it to intend THE FUTURE VISIBLE REIGN OF
MESSIAH IN GLORY FOR A THOUSAND YEARS.

The proofs that generally the phrase does so mean, are
such as the following :—

1. The idea of the " kingdom of heaven," it is agreed,
is taken from the prophecies of Daniel.

i. "And in the days of these (ten) kings shall *the God of
heaven* set up a *kingdom,* which shall never be destroyed : and
the kingdom shall not be left to other people, but it shall break
in pieces and consume all these kingdoms, and it shall stand for
ever : " Dan. ii, 44.

ii. Nebuchadnezzar was driven from men because of his
attributing his dominion to himself : he was restored to it, " after
he should have known *that the heavens do rule :* " iv, 26.

iii. " The same horn made war with the saints and prevailed
against them ; until the Ancient of Days came, and judgment
was given to the saints of the Most High, (or rather, ' to the saints
of the *heavenly places :* ') and the time came that *the saints
possessed the kingdom :* " vii, 21, 22.

2. From these and similar passages of the prophets,
the Jews were expecting that dominion should be given to
themselves over all the nations of the earth ; and that
Messiah should be their prince, ruling at Jerusalem. This
is granted by all. But it appears also, from several passages
of the New Testament that while they were mistaken in
supposing themselves the saints to whom the kingdom was
promised, they were yet right in their main expectations.

i. " Then said Jesus unto his disciples, Verily I say unto you,
that a rich man shall *hardly enter the kingdom of heaven.* And

again I say unto you, it is easier for a camel to go through the eye of a needle, than for a rich man to *enter into the kingdom of God.*" " Then answered Peter and said unto him, behold we have forsaken all and followed thee ; what shall we have therefore ? And Jesus said unto them, Verily I say unto you, that ye which have followed me, *in the regeneration when the Son of man shall sit on the throne of his glory, ye also shall sit upon twelve thrones, judging the twelve tribes of Israel :* " Matt. xix, 23, 24, 27, 28.

ii.   The mother of James and John petitions Christ, that her " *two sons might sit, the one on thy right hand and the other on thy left, in thy kingdom.*" Jesus, in his reply, would teach them that they knew not, in asking for such a boon, how much of suffering must be endured, before such a post could be attained. He adds also, that such places of dignity were not at his own disposal, but already decreed by the Father: Matt. xx, 20-23.

iii.   " And when one of them that sat at meat with him heard these things, he said unto him, *Blessed is he that shall eat bread in the kingdom of God :*" Luke xiv, 15. Jesus takes up his words, and intimates that while it would be blessed, yet that men in general would not regard the invitation to that banquet of God.

iv.   It is in virtue of such general agreement with the thoughts of the Jewish nation, that the Jews are called " *the children of the kingdom :*" (Matt. vii, 12) though for their unbelief the majority would be cast out.

3.   The kingdom is spoken of as still *future :* the Gospel stands related to it only as the *invitation* does to the *feast.*

1.   " *Thy kingdom come :*" Luke xi, 2.

ii.   " The law and the prophets were until John : since that time the kingdom of God *is being preached,* and every one is pressing into it : " Luke xvi, 16.

iii.   In the parable of the wedding supper all that is supposed to be done, is the collecting of guests for the feast. The feast begins not till all are assembled, and till the king has come in, and put out the unfit guests : Matt. xxii.

4.   The Transfiguration was a type of the kingdom. The kingdom is to be set up at Jesus' return in glory.

i.   When Peter had confessed Jesus as the Son of the living God in the name of his fellow-apostles, Jesus foretells the future erection of his church, and its resurrection from the gates of *Hades,* (not, ' *of hell.*') He then promised to Peter the keys of the kingdom of heaven, and foretells his own death. He fore-warns the disciple, that his career must be one of suffering like his Master's. But what then ? Even martyrdom, far from being an obstacle to entrance into the kingdom, should admit into it. " For whosoever shall save his life shall lose it : *and whosoever shall lose his life for my sake shall find it.*" And when shall that be ? " *The Son of man shall come in the glory of his Father with his angels ;* and then shall he reward each* according to his works. Verily I say unto you, there be some standing here, which shall not taste of death till they shall *see the Son of man coming in his kingdom :* " Matt. xvi, 13—28.†

Then follows, in each of the gospels, an account of the Transfiguration. That scene is, therefore, a type of the coming kingdom of Messiah, when the dead saints and the living shall both meet in the presence of Christ, and the Father's voice of attestation and of joy shall go forth, while his brightness encircles the whole.

5. The kingdom of God is spoken of as the time of reward for the persecuted in this life.

i. " *Blessed are they which have been* (Greek) *persecuted for righteousness' sake ; for theirs is the kingdom of heaven.* Blessed are ye when men shall revile you and persecute you, and shall say all manner of evil against you falsely for my sake. Rejoice, and be exceeding glad, for great is your reward in heaven : " Matt. v. 11, 12.

ii. " Confirming the souls of the disciples, and exhorting them to continue in the faith, and that *we must through much tribulation enter into the kingdom of God :* " Acts xiv, 22.

The disciples were already within the church and believers in the Gospel. But they had yet to enter the kingdom, which is set before them as their hope.

iii. " We ourselves glory in you in the churches of God for your patience and faith in all your persecutions and tribulation that ye endure, which is a manifest token of the righteous judg-ment of God, *that ye may be counted worthy of the kingdom of God, for which ye even suffer · *" 2 Thess. i, 4, 5.

* Εκαστῳ.

†So Luke xxii, 42. It should be, " When thou comest *in* thy kingdom," not 'into.'

iv. "I was delivered out of the mouth of the lion. And the Lord shall deliver me from every evil work, *and will preserve me unto his heavenly kingdom:*" 2 Tim. iv, 18.

6. The circumstances of it prove it to be the kingdom of glory. It is to be at Christ's return, at the last trump.

i. "The Son of man shall send forth his angels and they shall gather out of *his kingdom* all stumbling-blocks* *and them which do iniquity:* and shall cast them into the furnace of fire; there shall be wailing and gnashing of teeth. *Then shall the righteous shine forth as the sun in the kingdom of their Father·*" Matt. xiii, 41—43.

ii. "I will not drink henceforth of this fruit of the vine until *that day when I drink it new with you in my Father's kingdom.*" Matt. xxvi, 29.

iii. "With desire I have desired to eat this passover with you before I suffer, *For I say unto you, I will not any more eat thereof, until it be fulfilled in the kingdom of God:*" Luke xxii, 15, 16.

iv. "Ye are they which have continued with me in my temptations, and I appoint *unto you a kingdom, as my Father hath appointed unto me, that ye may eat and drink at my table in my kingdom, and sit on thrones judging the twelve tribes of Israel:*" Luke xxiii, 28—30.

The employment shows that the time of grace is not meant, but the season of glory after the resurrection.

The kingdom of heaven then† is the millennial glory appointed for Christ.

But there is one exception to this use of the expression which is often quoted. The Pharisees inquired of the Saviour, "When is the kingdom of God coming?" To which he replied, "The kingdom of God is not coming with observation, (watching,) neither shall they say, 'Lo here,' or 'lo there,' for behold the kingdom of God is within you·" Luke xvii, 20, 21.

In the above words, our Lord refers the Pharisees to the

* Σκανδαλα.

†It is confessed, that "the kingdom *of God*," has a somewhat different meaning from the phrase, "the kingdom *of heaven;*" but the difference is not such as to interfere with the present question.

necessary internal preparation of the soul, without which, inquiry into the outward and future kingdom was but curious folly. But this was a reply only to the cavillers and ungodly, not to his believing people. To *them*, in the next verses, he proceeds to speak of it as future and visible, declaring that at his return he would blaze forth in majesty filling from end to end the sky, like the lightning.

We have now to prove, that the kingdom is a time of *reward :* and that the *entrance into it will turn upon the conduct of the believer.*

i. So connected is one part of the subject with another, that some of the passages already adduced present a portion of the evidence. In Matthew xvi, Jesus, after foretelling his own death, invites the disciples to follow him even unto death, promising that life so lost shall be found again in the kingdom. " For the Son of man shall come in the glory of his Father, *and then shall he reward each according to his works."* He closes with a promise to give a sight of his *kingdom* to some then present before they should die.

ii. In connexion with this we may take the passage which more especially affirms, that the duration of the kingdom shall be for a thousand years. There the martyrs for Christ's sake specially appear : Rev. xx, 4.

iii. " The seventh angel sounded, and there were great voices in heaven, saying, *The kingdoms* of this world are become the kingdoms of our Lord and of his Christ."* Thereupon the elders say before God, " Thy wrath is come, and the time of the dead that they should be judged, *and that thou shouldest give* THE REWARD† *unto thy servants the prophets, and to the saints, and to them that fear thy name, small and great :* " Rev. xi, 15—18.

As it is the kingdom *of the saints,* those who enter must be holy ones.

i. " *Not every one that saith unto me Lord, Lord, shall enter into the kingdom of heaven ; but he that doeth the will of my Father which is in heaven.* Many will say unto me in that day, Lord, Lord, have we not prophesied in thy name ? and in thy name cast out devils ? and in thy name done many wonderful works ? And then will I profess unto them, I never knew you ; depart from me, *ye that work iniquity :* " Matt. vii, 21—23.

*The best MSS. read " kingdom." † Τον μισθον.

ii. " Now the works of the flesh are manifest, which are these, adultery, fornication, uncleanness, lasciviousness, idolatry, hatred, variance, emulations, wrath, strife, seditions, heresies, envyings, murder, drunkenness, revellings, and such like, of the which I tell you before, as I have also told you in time past, *that they which do such things shall not inherit the kingdom of God :* " Gal. v, 19—21.

It is set before the disciple as the object of his desire and striving.

i. " Therefore take no thought (be not anxious), saying, " What shall we eat ? or what shall we drink ? or wherewithal shall we be clothed ? *But seek ye first the kingdom of God*, and his righteousness, and all these things shall be added unto you · " Matt. vi, 31—33.

ii. " From the days of John the Baptist until now, the kingdom of heaven is suffering violence, and violent ones are taking it by force : " (*See Greek.*) Matt. xi, 12.

iii. " Fear not little flock, for it is your Father's good pleasure to give you the kingdom. Sell that ye have and give alms, provide yourself bags which wax not old, a treasure in the heavens, that fadeth not : " Luke xii, 32, 33.

iv. " Beside this, giving all diligence, add to your faith virtue ; and to virtue knowledge ; and to knowledge temperance : and to temperance patience ; and to patience godliness ; and to godliness brotherly kindness ; and to brotherly kindness charity ; (love). For if these things be in you and abound they make you that ye shall neither be idle (*marg.*) nor unfruitful in the knowledge of our Lord Jesus Christ . . . . *Wherefore the rather, brethren, give diligence to make your calling and election sure : for if ye do these things, ye shall never fail, for so the entrance* (Gr.) *shall be ministered to you abundantly into the everlasting kingdom of our Lord and Saviour Jesus Christ :* " 2 Pet. i, 5—11.

Here the kingdom is called " everlasting," and so it is, in one view, for those who reign the thousand years shall also reign " for ever and ever : " Rev. xx, 4 ; xxii, 5.

v. " *Whosoever therefore shall break one of these least commandments, and shall teach men so, he shall be called the least in the kingdom of heaven : but whosoever shall do and teach them, the same shall be called great in the kingdom of heaven :* " Matt. v, 19.

Several passages already quoted discover how closely connected are the resurrection and the kingdom. The

Saviour then advises his disciples to seek their reward, not now, but in the kingdom

vi. " Take heed that ye do not your alms before men, to be seen of them, *otherwise ye have no reward of you*r *Father which is in heaven.*" The Pharisees did theirs to be seen : they *had their reward* in the present life : Matt. vi, 1, 2. " Then said he also to him that bade him, When thou makest a dinner or supper call not thy friends nor thy brethren, neither thy kinsmen, nor thy rich neighbours, *lest they also bid thee again, and a recompense be made thee.* But when thou makest a feast, call the poor, the maimed, the lame, the blind, and thou shalt be blessed, *for they cannot recompense thee, for thou shalt be recompensed at the resurrection of the just :* " Luke xiv, 12—14.

7. On the ground of reward according to works, the living heathen nations of the globe receive their part in the kingdom, or are cast out.

" Then shall the king say to them on his right hand, *Come ye blessed of my Father, inherit the kingdom* prepared for you from the foundation of the world : FOR *I was an hungred, and ye gave me meat : I was thirsty, and ye gave me drink : I was a stranger, and ye took me in : naked, and ye clothed me : sick, and ye visited me : I was in prison, and ye came unto me :* " Matt. xxv, 34—36.

The tracing out these truths will fully repay the student of Holy Scripture.

It is owing to the different footing on which the Most High has set *eternal life* on the one hand, and the *kingdom of God* on the other, that the Epistle to the Romans stands so contrasted with that to the Hebrews.

The grand subject of the Romans is, THE RIGHTEOUSNESS PROVIDED BY GOD. The apostle first manifests the necessity of righteousness ; because God has proclaimed himself the enemy of all unrighteousness. He is the avenger of offences against himself and mankind.

But the heathen are guilty of both kinds of transgression, and condemned by their own consciences.

Nor do the Jews stand on higher ground. They offend against greater light than the Gentiles, and are guilty before both God and man. The just condemnation of all the world is then proved by scripture quotations. There is therefore none deserving of eternal life, either among Jews or Gentiles. Hereupon the Holy Spirit develops the righteousness provided for the guilty by the imputed obedience and death of Christ, which is appropriated by faith: Ch. i, ii, iii.

Even Abraham was justified by faith, and not by his circumcision, or by his obedience generally: Ch. iv. In chap. v, God's provision for the saint's access to him, the love that furnished the ransom, and our joy in receiving it are set forth. Then appears our condemnation in Adam, ere actual sin broke out in us personally. Thus our justification in Christ by faith answers to our condemnation in Adam.

Chap. vi: But does not the view of our passiveness, and of God's grace abounding to remedy sin, open the door to living in iniquity? No: the Christian scheme presents baptism as its next demand to faith, and baptism represents death to sin. In this view the Christian is exhorted by Paul to act up to the emblematic picture exhibited in that rite. Baptism represents death to the old husband—the law: life to the new husband—Christ: Ch. vii.

The certainty of the believer's standing is then discovered to us, in the Spirit's aid, in God's eternal purpose, and in his efficient agency put forth, making all things turn to the advantage of the elect. Herein the saints are passive. God selects whom he wills, before any deed of good or evil wrought. But if man be so passive, is not God unjust? Nay, God has the right of the potter to make vessels of honour or dishonour. Israel's stumbling was long ago foreseen, foretold of God, and foreordained to his glory: Chaps. viii, ix.

But yet a sufficient reason for Israel's casting off is also found, in their rejection of this righteousness provided in Christ: ix, 30—33. The true position of faith then appears.

It is not working to obtain a future righteousness of its own, but it simply welcomes the one provided and finished of God. The faithless activity of the Jews to maintain their own righteousness is contrasted with the passiveness of the Gentile elect. " I was found *of them that sought me not. I was made manifest to them that asked not after me* · " x, 20.

Israel's fall is due to God's sovereignty ; but their fall is only partial, and temporary. The promises of God to the nation ensure its final restoration : Ch. xi.

The rest of the epistle is practical direction to those who had accepted the righteousness of God.

Thus the Epistle to the Romans gives us THE CERTAINTY OF ETERNAL LIFE AS CONNECTED WITH GOD'S PREDESTINATING GRACE TO HIS ELECT.

It exhibits three aspects of eternal life answerable to the views above given.

1. It is set before man on fulfilment of certain conditions. It testifies of " the day of wrath and revelation of the righteous judgment of God, *who will render to every man according to his deeds. To them who by patient continuance in well doing seek for glory and honour and immortality,* ETERNAL LIFE. But unto them that are contentious, and do not obey the truth, but obey unrighteousness, indignation and wrath, tribulation and anguish, upon every soul of man that doeth evil : " Rom. ii, 5—9.

2. It discovers eternal life as deserved by the second Adam, and freely given to believers.

" That as sin reigned unto death, even so might *grace reign through righteousness unto* ETERNAL LIFE *by Jesus Christ our Lord* : " Rom. v, 21.

Hence the justification introduced by Jesus is called in a former verse " justification of life," that is, justification bringing eternal life.

3. " Therefore, as by the offence of one, judgment came upon all men unto condemnation, even so by the righteousness of one the free gift came *unto** all men unto *justification of life :* " v, 18.

Lastly, it sums up the matter strikingly in one sentence.

" *For the wages of sin is death,* but THE GIFT OF GOD IS ETERNAL LIFE, *by Jesus Christ our Lord :* " vi, 23.

As then faith is the gift of God, bestowed on a certain number by his predestinating grace, eternal life is secure for all the elect, and the apostle challenges the universe to hinder their attaining it : Rom. viii. " It is of faith, that it might be by grace, *to the end the promise might be made sure to all the seed ;* " Rom. iv, 16.

These topics connect together strongly the Gospel of John and the Epistle to the Romans.

But the Epistle to the Hebrews gives quite a contrasted view. It allies itself with the second truth developed in this tract. Its burthen is, the necessity of effort to secure the entrance into the kingdom of God. Its exhortations turn mainly on the danger of being shut out ; a danger which will in many cases be realized.

In a succeeding chapter, this view of the Hebrews will be dealt with in detail. But for the present, it will suffice to exhibit some topics found in the two Epistles, in order to prove to the reader the remarkable contrasts which they form to one another.

The Romans gives us *God's work, his* plans, *his* power, *his* sovereignty of choice, the security of his elect.

The Hebrews gives us *God's just demands* of those whom he has made partakers of his grace : and the equity of his awards, as manifested in his past judgments.

How great the contrast of such passages as these ! " We know that all things work together for good to them that

---

* Εἰς παντας. The rendering " upon " introduces error. The justification of Christ is present *unto* all, but it is only *upon* the believer.

love God, to them who are the called according to his purpose. For whom he did foreknow, he did also predestinate . . . . . Moreover, whom he did predestinate, them he also called : and whom he called, them he also justified : and whom he justified, them he also glorified : " Rom. viii, 28—30.

" Whose house are we, IF we hold fast the confidence and the rejoicing of the hope firm unto the end. Wherefore (as the Holy Ghost saith), ' To-day IF ye will hear his voice harden not your hearts : ' " Heb. iii, 6, 7.

" Take heed, brethren, LEST there be *in any of you* an evil heart of unbelief in departing from the living God. But exhort one another daily, while it is called to-day, LEST *any of you* be hardened through the deceitfulness of sin. For we are made partakers (associates) of Christ, IF we hold the beginning of our confidence steadfast unto the end : " Heb. iii, 12—14.

" If " and " lest " are words inwoven into the chief passages of the Hebrews, ıı, 1 ; iv, 1, 11 ; xii, 3, 13 ; x, 38.

In Romans it is—eternal life or death to the receivers or rejectors of the righteousness of God. In Hebrews it is—reward or loss to those already accepted before the Most High. God in Hebrews presents himself as " the REWARDER of those who diligently seek him," and his servants are the men of faith, having " respect unto the recompense of reward : " Heb. x, 35 ; xi, 6, 26. Hence too, the necessity of pleasing him is introduced several times : Heb. x, 38, ; xi, 5, 6 ; xii, 16, 28 ; xiii, 21.

1. Both Epistles refer to ABRAHAM.

In Romans, he is set before our eyes as the pattern of the justified ; not received on the ground of his obedience and good works, but *accounted righteous by believing*, against the suggestions of nature, the power of God to raise the dead.

In Hebrews, on the other hand, he is the pattern to those already received of God, on the ground of *active obedience after his justification:* (Heb. vi, 11—18), by which he at length obtained the oath of God.

In Hebrews the reference is to Abraham offering up his Son (Gen. xxii); as in Romans the reference was to his simple act of faith, as recorded (Gen. xv).

2. In both Epistles the history of ESAU is commented on.

In Romans it is—Esau the *passive*—rejected ere he had done good or evil, by the sovereignty of the Supreme Disposer.

" And not only this; but when Rebecca also had conceived by one, even by our father Isaac (for the children being not yet born, neither having done either good or evil, that the purpose of God according to election might stand, not of works, but of him that calleth); it was said unto her, the elder shall serve the younger. As it was written, Jacob have I loved, *but Esau have I hated*" : Rom. ix, 13.

In Hebrews it is—Esau the *responsible*—dealt with according to his ungoldly choice, held up by the apostle as an example to be shunned by believers. " Looking diligently lest any fail of the grace of God : lest any root of bitterness springing up trouble you, and thereby many be defiled; lest any be a *fornicator, or profane person as Esau*, who for a single meal* sold his birth-right. For ye know how that afterward, when he would have inherited the blessing, he was rejected; for he found no place of repentance, though he sought it earnestly with tears " : Heb. xii, 16, 17.

3. The history of ISRAEL occurs in both; but from opposite points of view.

In Romans it is Israel's rejection for an appointed time by the Most High, according to his prophecies.

In Hebrews it is, Israel's exclusion from the promised

* Bowσις.

land, as the due recompense of their shutting their ears, hardening their hearts, and provoking God ; Heb. iii.

4. THE KINGDOM, or the glory of the Millennium, enters into both Epistles, but with similar contrasts.

In Romans it is an object to be patiently waited for, in the spirit of the groaning, but patiently tarrying creation. If new created by the Holy Ghost and joint sufferers with Christ, we shall have part in " the manifestation of the sons of God."

In Hebrews, on the other hand, it is a rest proposed to the people of God, which is to be entered into by diligent obedience to God. " LET US LABOUR THEREFORE TO ENTER INTO THAT REST, *lest any fall after the same example* OF DISOBEDIENCE* " · Heb. iv, 11.

These observations will, I trust, suffice to show the importance of accepting both these principles.

It is necessary to our present peace to acknowledge the righteousness of Christ, without works of ours, imputed by God to all believers. It is necessary to present joy that we embrace the assurance of our eternal life as already begun, and with certainty to be accomplished in eternity, in spite of all resistance on the part of creatures. Believers in *the Sovereignty of God* alone will feel themselves in full sympathy with the apostle's letter to Rome.

But to be in sympathy with the letter to the Hebrews we must receive the doctrine of *God's Justice,* as hereafter to be applied to the conduct of *believers.* We must admit, that the entrance into Messiah's kingdom of the thousand years is a prize to be won or lost according to our works, ere the arguments and exhortations to the Hebrew Christians can be understood, or will rightly affect our practice.

May God grant to his saints earnestly and candidly to weigh the statements here propounded : and to search the Scriptures, to see if these things are so.

* Απειθειας.

CHAPTER SECOND.

THE PRIZE OF OUR CALLING.

PHILIPPIANS III.

In considering the difference between the conditions on which eternal life, and the kingdom of God respectively are set, the testimony of the Holy Spirit in the third chapter of Philippians is very important. Let us contemplate it then.

1. "Finally, my brethren, rejoice in the Lord. To write the same things to you, to me indeed is not grievous, but for you it is safe. 2. Beware of the dogs, beware of the evil workmen,* beware of the concision. 3. For we are the circumcision, who worship God in the Spirit† and boast in Christ Jesus‡ and have no confidence in the flesh."

The apostle, by exhorting them to rejoice in Christ, sounds the key note to the topic which instantly succeeds. The Judaizing teachers called them to trust in their own natural powers and merits. The man of the law has confidence in himself. The son of the gospel must trust in the Lord his righteousness, as the prophet had before taught: Isa. xlv, 25.

At Philippi, as elsewhere, there were, as it would seem, Jewish zealots, who sought to introduce circumcision and

---

* The article before both.
† Some critics read, πνευματί Θεου.
‡ Καυχωμενοι.

the keeping of the law, as in part, if not altogether, the ground of their justification. All but the circumcised they regarded as Gentile " dogs " and persecuted the disciples of Jesus, if they refused to comply with their demands. Against such Paul drops the word of caution. He completely turns the tables on them. *They*, not believers in Jesus, were the " dogs " now.* They were, like that animal, unclean, and unaccepted before God.

They were also " evil workmen." They were not idlers ; but they sought to build up the false doctrine, and to pull down the true.' Professing themselves Moses' disciples, they resisted the authority of Messiah, the Lord of Moses.

Thrice he repeats, " Beware ! " In a world of evil, danger takes many forms. This repeated admonition refers to the same parties under different aspects. Let the church of Christ beware of the literal circumcision, and of its professors. It was not, indeed, properly to be called " circumcision " now ; for God had departed from the form. Its covenant, its standing, and rites, ever since Messiah had appeared, if taken alone, were deadly. God had left the shadow, for the substance had come. The spirit of the law was gone ; it was now but the corpse. He could only call therefore its initiatory rite, by the name of " mutilation," or " mangling."

Believers are now the true circumcision. They, like Abraham, only in fuller measure, have seen Messiah and His day, and are glad. They have Abraham's spirit of faith, and Christ is to them the fulfilment of the law ; which is better than being sons of Arbaham's flesh, and of the law of Moses, which condemns all. They are the worshippers in spirit and in truth, whom the Father is now seeking. The Jew knew and regarded only the outward act, and despised and railed at the inward reality. Circumcised in flesh, he was uncircumcised in heart. Seeking

*Probably there is a reference to Isa. lvi, 10, 11.

to establish his own righteousness, he was a despiser of the righteousness sent by God through Jesus Christ.

Against circumcision, then, and the teachers of it, the church of Christ is warned. Its principles are alien to those of Christ. But the advocates of infant baptism are teachers of circumcision. The covenant of circumcision, which is the law, is their main stronghold against the baptism of believers.* While they do not plead for the *act* of circumcision to be added to the gospel ground of justification, as did the Jewish teachers of old they do plead for the *laws* of circumcision, as a fitting or necessary supplement to those of Christ. But in so doing, they are pleading for the addition of the law and the flesh, to the pure gospel of Christ. Many of them indeed are holy men, and useful in other respects ; and they do this in ignorance. They would sooner cut off their hand than hinder the gospel. To such then we lift up the voice of testimony. If the infants of believers be nearer to God than other infants, it must be because the flesh of believers is better than other flesh. And then, just to this extent, " confidence in the flesh " is brought in ; a thing against which the Holy Spirit here declares himself. The true circumcision puts " *no* confidence in the flesh." In all alike, the flesh is equally worthless and dead.

4. " Although I am in possession† of ground of confidence even in the flesh. If any other thinketh of trusting in the flesh, I more. 5. Circumcised the eighth day, of the race of Israel, of the tribe of Benjamin, an Hebrew of Hebrews, concerning the law, a Pharisee. 6. Concerning zeal, persecuting the church ; concerning righteousness that is in the law, having been blameless."‡

These words indirectly meet an objection likely to occur to the mind. One sometimes finds persons very

---

*See this subject treated in ' *Baptism and the Abrahamic Covenant.*'

† Εχων πεποιθησιν και εν σαρκι.

‡ Literally, ' having become ' ; γενομενος.

vehement in condemnation of qualities, stations, or advantages, which they do not possess, and cannot obtain for themselves. The possessors of these things then turn upon their heels with a smile at such condemnation; and say, with the proverb, "The grapes are sour." Paul therefore, to manifest that such was not the reason of his speaking so strongly against the righteousness of the law, discovers to us that he condemned that ground of hope, though he was himself in possession of it in its fullest extent. There was no one who could exceed him in such boasting, as far as the circumstances of his birth, education, and personal obedience were concerned. He glories in seven points, which again are divided into four and three · he was—

1. "Circumcised the eighth day."

This was the day demanded by the covenant of circumcision with Abraham, and afterwards reaffirmed by the law of Moses.

2. "Of the race of Israel."

Circumcision was practised by Ishmael and his race, and by the Edomites, as well as by Israel and his descendants. But Paul was not a proselyte, but by birth one of the chosen nation.

3. "Of the tribe of Benjamin."

Benjamin was one of the two tribes that abode with the house of David, when the other ten severed themselves.

4. "An Hebrew of Hebrews."

His family had ever kept itself separate from mixture with the Gentiles, when so many had intermarried with the heathen around.

Here the first division ends.

The law sets each individual who would be saved by it, on his own merits singly. "The *man* that doeth them shall live by them." Paul therefore, when presenting his hopes from the law, dwells entirely on his individual standing. He boasts in the flesh. His boasts take in his (1) nation, (2) tribe, (3) family, and (4) his own personal initiation as a babe.

The three last boasts all commence with the same word,* and regard his choice, and mode of life, when come to years of discretion.

5. " According to the law, a Pharisee."

He had been educated in the strictest principles of orthodoxy, and had ever retained them. He added to the observances required by the Law, the traditions demanded by the elders.

6. " According to zeal, persecuting the church."

This, which he elsewhere states as his greatest sin, here appears as one of his merits ; for he is reckoning now as the Jewish teachers did. His reverence and admiration for the law of Moses were such, that he sought to overthrow whatever stood in opposition thereto.

7. " According to righteousness which is in the law, having been blameless."

He was not one excommunicated by the Pharisees ; not one, who, after expulsion becoming a renegade, turns round with fury upon the party that have disowned, or expelled him. As far as the outward observances which the law required went, the apostle's life was blameless. His opponents could allege against him no instance of infraction of the Mosaic code.

7. " But what things were gain to me, those I counted loss for the Christ. 8. Yea, doubtless, and I count all things to be loss for the excellency of the knowledge of Christ Jesus my Lord, for whom I suffered the loss of all things, and I account them to be dung, that I might win Christ. 9. And be found in him, not having mine own righteousness which is from the law, but that (which is) by faith in Christ† the righteousness which is from God upon faith."‡ (Greek).

* Κατα.　　　† Literally, ' of Christ.'　　　‡ Επι τη πιστει.

Justification by our own works keeps us alone : but the Spirit takes us out of ourselves, takes away both from our good and evil works, and unites us to the Messiah, making all His fulness our ground of confidence. His obedience to law, His death for sin, become ours. To obtain this, Paul gladly surrenders his own boasts of himself. He casts away his old confidence. " What things were gain to me, those I counted loss in comparison of the Messiah."

Herein see the wisdom of God ! It is not the uncircumcised Gentile who treads underfoot circumcision and the law, but the *Pharisee ;* one who could boast of righteousness by obedience to law. This is the man whom the Spirit of God selects, to teach us the real worthlessness of the greatest merits of the law ; and the superiority of that better righteousness which is brought in by the life and death of the Second Adam.

As soon as the apostle discerned the glory of the righteousness provided for sinners in the Son of God, he regarded all his former jewels as dung. The labour of his life was vanity. Justly did he so regard it. Had he seen the way of faith of which the psalms and prophets, and even the law spoke, he would have perceived the impossibility of being justified by his own deeds before a perfectly just and holy God. He would have been looking forward to Messiah, and the complete righteousness promised in him. Being thus justified by faith, like Abraham his father, he would have been accepted by God. But now he saw that all his life was vain, since it had been spent under the guidance of a false principle.

Not only did he think so, under the first discovery of his own guilt before the demands of the law upon the heart ; but he thought so still. Everything which either the Jew or Gentile could possess of goodness, power, knowledge, he regarded as dung in comparison of the superior knowledge of the Messiah Jesus, whom he confessed his Master and Lord.

By professing faith in Jesus as the Messiah, he lost entirely his wordly position among his countrymen ; but he was well content. He esteemed these objects of earthly desire, not only as trifles, but as loathsome. His heart was set on Messiah. His choice was the choice of God. He saw that beauty in Jesus, in a measure, which the Father perceives in its fulness. He saw, and the sight deadened him to every other object to admiration. Thus does Paul exhibit himself as the merchantman of the parable, who, after seeing the one perfect pearl, gladly exchanged his former pearls, and all that he had, to obtain that.

He would gain Messiah, and the righteousness which is in him. But in order to be justified by Christ, it is necessary to be one with him. Hence he adds, " And be found *in him*." Having once been united to Christ, there must we abide, there be "*found*" in the great day. As the Israelite was safe only in the blood-sprinkled house, and was commanded to abide there till the morning lest the sword should find him outside, so he who is in Christ, is required to abide in Him.

The above verses contain a formal renunciation of all merits in himself, all claim for reward from any obedience he had rendered to the law. He then chooses the righteousness which is obtained by believing in Jesus as the Messiah, the appointed Righteousness of the people of God. This is very clearly set forth. The righteousness is thrice defined—First, what it is *not*, " Not having mine own righteousness which is from law." Secondly, " that which is *by faith in Christ*." This teaches us the mode in which it becomes ours. Thirdly, " the righteousness which is from God upon faith." It is righteousness "*from* God," in opposition to the justice of God, the righteousness which is *in* Him. It is " upon faith." This may have

two meanings ; both of which are true. " Upon faith,"
in regard to *time,* so that the moment a man believes,
he is justified. So we say, " *Upon* your laying down a
thousand pounds, the house is yours." Or the reterence
may be to a vesture cast *upon* the shoulders Then
this righteousness abides " upon faith," as its perpetual
clothing.

Thus we have the first part of the knowledge of
Messiah. " By his *knowledge* (or the knowledge of him)
shall my righteous servant *justify* many, for he shall
bear their iniquities." Up to this point believers have
ever gone.

The knowledge of Messiah as His righteousness was
Paul's first step towards the kingdom of God. His former
righteousness, as the Saviour declared, could not win
him an entrance there. It was but the righteousness of
the Pharisee ; and Jesus assured the Jew solemnly, that
without some better righteousness than that, none should
be admitted thither : Matt. v, 20.

Having now, however, received God's perfect righteousness, with the hand of faith, he was at peace with God,
and dead to the law. But that step was only the beginning
of a new life ; with a new prize set before him. The
object exhibited to the eye of one under the Law, was, to
earn *eternal life* by strict obedience to the whole law.
Failure on a single point, and that, tested by rigorous justice,
drew down eternal death : Matt. xix, 16, 19. But eternal
life is *given* to the believer at once on faith : Rom. vi, 23.
What then is the new prize for which he is to strive ?
The subsequent verses inform us.

10. " That I may know him, and the power of his resurrection, and the fellowship of his sufferings, being conformed to
his death, if by any means I might attain to the select resurrection from among the dead."*

*The critical editions read, with very remarkable emphasis.
Την εξαναστασιν την εκ νεκρων.

The verse before us stands connected with verse eight ; the intermediate parts being a parenthesis. " I count them all loss for the excellency of the *knowledge* of Christ (for whom I suffered the loss of all   . that I might win Christ . . the righteousness from God which is upon faith) that I may *know* him," etc.

The first knowledge of Christ as His righteousness gave peace with God. But there was a further knowledge, continually unfolding in the future, which the apostle desired. It was an experimental knowledge ; of the person, work, and mind, of the acts, prophecies, and pro- mises of Christ. This was communicated in a high and blissful degree then, by immediate inspiration. To this the Christian should pray to attain now ; for the promises of the gifts then granted do not belong to those times alone I Cor. xiv, 1.

He wished to know also " the power of his resurrection." This is attainable, and to be sought by the Christian in the present life. He is to seek fully to realize his position, as one with Christ. As united to Him, he is dead to the earth, and the things of it. He is risen with Christ, and spiritually seated with him on high. In the strength of his new life, he is to overcome the deeds of the flesh. " I live, yet not I, but Christ liveth in me." By the power of Jesus in resurrection, we are enabled to live as those dead to sin, and alive to God through Christ ; as those who are risen men, passing through earth by the light and principles of heaven.

But this spirit of Christ acted out in life brings us into collision with the spirit and ways of the world ; and there- fore into conflict and suffering. Thus it was with our Lord. Thus it hates *us*, if we resemble our Master. Sufferings thence arising, and met in the spirit of Christ, are " the fellowship of his sufferings."

These Paul desired. So great is the joy promised to suffering with Christ, that the apostle welcomed it. Nay,

so excellent did the glory of the prize set before him appear,
that he even coveted martyrdom, as the way thereto.
" If we suffer (with Christ) we shall also reign with him."
" He that loseth his life for my sake shall find it." So sure
did he reckon this promise, and so blessed its fulfilment,
that he desired to lay down his life for Christ's sake. That
way had the Master led : that path would the disciple
follow. Herein he was superior, in intelligence and grace,
to Peter as we see him in the Gospels. When Jesus had
received Peter's confession of Himself as the Son of the
living God, He prophesies His own rejection by the people
of Israel even unto death. Peter, staggered at the idea
so contrary to his Jewish prepossessions, rebuked the
Saviour ; and was in turn rebuked, as relishing the things
of the flesh alone, and not those of God. Then the Re-
deemer added, that the path of the disciple all the way to
the kingdom was to be, like His own, one of rejection and
suffering from an evil world. This Paul perceives and
welcomes. He embraced the cross, as at once the ground
of his justification, and the symbol of his life. He was
ambitious to tread in the steps of his Divine Master. Like
some young soldier of old, smitten with the view of David's
faith and prowess against Goliath, and persuaded that he
was the anointed heir to the crown, he sought to follow
in the steps of Christ, though they led through scenes of
trial and danger. Paul saw too—what the sons of Zebedee
beheld not—that the places of glory in Messiah's Kingdom
were to be granted to those who had suffered greatly
for Christ : Matt. xx, 20-23. " Rejoice, inasmuch as ye
are partakers of Christ's sufferings, that ye may also rejoice
with exceeding joy, when his glory shall be revealed " ·
1 Pet. iv, 13.

The apostle desired to be conformed, even to the death
of Christ. Now, in one view of it, the death of the Lord
Jesus was that of a martyr, sacrificed for confessing the
obnoxious doctrine, that he was the King of the Jews,

and the Son of Man to whom the kingdom was promised.
Paul then actually coveted the martyr's death, as the
resemblance of that of the Lord Jesus, and as the certain
gate to the resurrection of the just. For the first resurrection is specially exhibited, as the assured portion of those
who have given up life in the service of Christ. " He that
loseth his life for my sake shall find it." Paul knew what
he sought ; and could with confidence surrender life itself,
the most valuable deposit of nature.

" If by any means I might attain to the resurrection
from among the dead."* It is evident at a glance, that
the resurrection which ·the apostle so earnestly sought,
was not the general resurrection. The wicked shall partake
of that, whether they desire it or not. Paul then could
not express any doubts of his attaining to that, or speak
of it as an object of hope. It remains then, that it be a
peculiar resurrection.: *the resurrection of reward*, obtained
by the just, while the wicked remain in their graves. Such
a resurrection we see in close connection with the kingdom
of Christ, and the time of reward : Rev. xi, 15–18 ; xx, 4.
The kingdom of Messiah, or that of the thousand years,
is entered by the door of " the first resurrection." All
who partake of that are blessed and holy ; kings and priests
of God and of Christ. So also the Saviour speaks of a
resurrection to which the sons of God alone would attain,
and of which God must account the partakers worthy :
Luke xx, 34–36.

Behold then the new hope, which the knowledge of
Jesus as the Messiah set before the eyes of the enlightened
apostle ! The Anointed One is to have companions in
the glory : Heb. i, 9 ; iii, 14. Paul's being already righteous by faith in the Lord's Anointed, entitled him to be a
runner for the prize. None can be admitted as a can- ◔
didate for reward, but he who is already accepted by grace

*The expression is peculiar, and may be rendered, " the
select resurrection from among the dead."

in the Beloved. But faith had brought Paul to the starting-post, and thenceforward his life was to be a pressing on for the crown.

The expression—"If by any means I might attain," —implies (1) the extreme eagerness of the apostle; (2) his sense of the value of the end he aimed at; and (3) the perception of the need of exertion, in order to realize the object of his pursuit.

Suffering, and the martyr's death, were as nothing to this divinely-enlightened mind, might he but attain "the first resurrection," the kingdom of the thousand years Rev. xx, 4. The hope, then, which spurred on the great apostle through every difficulty and danger, is now before us! Believer, seek to obtain that prize with like earnestness. *It is the hope of our calling!*

The zeal and endeavours of the apostle, conjoined with the implied possibility of loss, prove the solemn truth, *that some of the justified will not attain to it.* All the justified will receive *eternal life*, but not all will partake of the antepast of *the millennium.* For if diligence, earnestness, and careful heed to our words and deeds be necessary to obtain that reward, then the lukewarm and careless, the worldly, covetous, pleasure-loving, inconsistent Christian will not receive it. In the chapters which are to follow, the reader will see further and distincter proofs of this startling proposition.

We have now reached a position very different from that occupied at first. *Before*, it was justification, as the gift of God without works, possessed already by the simple believer in the merits of another. *Here*, it is works, effort, suffering, with a view to win something not ours as yet. Justification was Paul's at once on faith. The work of Jesus was perfect. He could not for a moment think of adding anything to the perfection of Christ. The prize, then, of the text is something quite distinct from eternal life. It is opened to faith in Messiah; it is intimately connected with His second coming. It is His promised kingdom. Faith brings at once eternal life. But, to one rightly instructed, faith is only the beginning of a life-long effort to attain the abundant entrance into the kingdom of God. So had the Saviour spoken of the kingdom. "It was suffering violence, and violent ones were taking it by force." It was not now the kingdom in its might, as discovered in the Jewish prophets, crushing all other kingdoms before it; but it was the *passive* object, the beleaguered city, whose walls he that would enter must scale. Jesus also, the King of that future empire, presents the same two-fold aspect. He is now the *passive* stone, on which we may build; on which the unbeliever falls, and is broken. He will be hereafter the *active* potent stone, descending from on high, which, if it fall upon his foes, will grind them to powder.

12. "Not that I have already received, or am already perfected; but I press forward, if indeed I may lay hold of that, for which I was also laid hold of by Christ Jesus. 13. Brethren, I do not reckon myself to have laid hold of it; but one thing I do, forgetting, on the one hand, the things behind, but stretching forth (on the other) after those in front, I press forward to the goal, for the prize of the heavenly calling of God in Christ Jesus."

The lesson for the Christian herein is close and solemn. So high were Paul's ideas of the requisites demanded of those who shall be privileged with entrance into that kingdom, that, in spite of all he had said, written, done, and suffered for the cause of Christ, he did not feel secure of his hope. And at what point of his course was he when he thus wrote? He had passed through the varied labours and endurances mentioned in the Acts of the Apostles; and was now a prisoner at Rome for the faith, in danger of death through the machinations of enemies. But if Paul thus thought of himself, who of *us* may flatter ourselves that we are safe? Still this is to be our aim. Our life after beginning to believe is either tending towards this, or from it. Each transgression tells against it ; till, if provocation is long continued, the patience of God is exhausted, the birthright is lost. Or, on the other hand, if the saint is consistent, and diligent in his course, at length the Most High irrevocably pledges Himself to give him the object of his pursuit. Such have obtained the promise—they are " perfected." But Paul thought not that it was his as yet. That word " already " implies, that he was on the right track, but that he deemed it enough if, at the close of his life, he should attain that assurance.

But this uncertainty had the right effect upon his mind and conduct. It but made him the more diligent. He represents himself as a racer, before whom a goal is set, the attaining of which would secure him the prize.

But not only was this Paul's desire, but it was the legitimate and authentic one. It was with a view to his attaining this, that Christ had laid hold of him. He was once wandering far from God. He had opposed himself to the knowledge of Christ. He had set himself to pluck up the faith by the roots. But, in the full enmity and aversion of his heart and of his way, Christ met and arrested him. Such was the fulness of divine *grace!* But the Lord then set him upon running a race for a *prize.* Behold the new principle of *reward according to works!* But was this Jesus' desire and design in Paul's case alone ? By no means. All believers are the " brethren " of the apostle in this respect, as he plainly declares afterwards. The prize, then, which Jesus proposes to the believer, and which He urges him to seek as the end of his conversion fully attained—is, *the being a participator in the millennial reign of the Messiah.*

Others, it would appear, deemed the great apostle sure of the end he proposed to himself, or rather which was proposed to him. But he says, I do not think so of *myself.* Thus we are introduced to a glimpse of another truth, more distinctly unfolded to us in another place,* that the judgment of the saints about us is a matter of comparatively small moment ; the real question being—What does *Christ* think of us ? *They* will not mete out the recompense, but Jesus alone. They judged, comparing this devoted servant of Christ with themselves, and others : but Paul measured himself by a far higher standard. " He that judgeth me is the Lord."

Perhaps too in the words, " I do not count myself to have apprehended," he hints obliquely at the security of some of the Philippian saints, as if they were sure of the prize. For it would seem, from some intimations of the epistle, that too high opinion of themselves was one of the few faults of that bright church.

The pursuit of this grand reward was His single object. " This one thing I do." Great excellence is to be attained only by directing our entire energies to a single object. Here we have Paul's. We are mercifully shown the main-spring, which moved his heart, and feet, and tongue. This one object swallowed up all others, and made him ever zealous, ever advancing, in the knowledge and love of Christ ; ever diligent in service, ever consistent with himself. Behold the motive which led him perpetually to brave the perils of a life devoted to preaching the Gospel ! Let not then such a discovery be made to us in vain. Let us take Paul's object—the object designed by the Lord Jesus to fill our hearts as believers ; and it cannot but quicken our steps in his ways.

Instead of falling back upon deeds of boldness, and on success already achieved, he forgot the past. Far from reposing on his laurels, he regarded not the things behind. He accounted nothing done, while aught re-mained to be accomplished. He was pressing onward still. The eager racer tarries not to see how much of the course is accomplished, but his eye is on the goal before him. Till that is reached, he will not pause. Though

*1 Cor. iv.

he bore the scars of many a well-fought field, he would not, if released from his present imprisonment, rest himself as a discharged veteran, from whom no more could be expected. No; he purposes still to go on, spreading the Gospel of the grace of God, a partaker of its afflictions *then*, that he might be a partaker of the glory of the Saviour *hereafter*. He *was* released; according to the hope he expresses in the epistle before us. He exerted himself anew, and was again arrested. We hear his last words in the second epistle to Timothy. But then he says, that *he now felt sure of the prize.* The goal was just won. He was about to yield up life itself in martyrdom for Christ; and he expresses his conviction at length, that Christ, when He should sit as *the righteous judge*, would award him the object of his so constant and persevering effort. " I am now ready to be offered, and the time of my departure is at hand. I have fought the good fight; I have finished the course; I have kept the faith; henceforth, there is laid up for me the crown of righteousness, which the Lord, the righteous judge, shall give me in that day, but not to me only, but unto them also which have loved His appearing " :* 2 Tim. iv, 6–8.

Paul pressed onward with a view to the prize. Whence it follows, that it is to be obtained as the result of effort, intelligent pursuit, suffering for Christ, advancement in grace. It is the end to which God has called the believer. It is " the prize of the high calling of God."† By " the *high* calling " is meant the same as " the *heavenly* calling " of Heb. iii, 1. It is God's call from on high up to Himself in heaven. Israel was called on earth to the things of earth. To be partakers then in the millennial kingdom of Christ is the joyful issue of a life of obedience to the heavenly call. " Ye are called in *one hope* of your calling "; and this is it. But the Holy Spirit saw how soon that end of a

*For the small differences of rendering, see the Greek.
† Της ανω κλησεως.

heavenly life would be obscured by the want of knowledge and faith in Christians. Paul prays, therefore, for the Ephesian saints, that "the eyes of their understanding being enlightened, *they might know what is the hope of his calling*": Eph. i, 18; iv. 1, 4. It is also entitled a "calling" to God's "kingdom and glory." Of *that* the apostle desired, that God would "*count them worthy*": 1 Thess. ii, 12; 2 Thess. i, 11; ii 14, The first chapter also of Peter's second epistle teaches us to endeavour to make sure, by a consistent life and advancing grace, our calling and election to the kingdom of our Lord and Saviour.

It is "the calling of God in Christ Jesus." That is, the call is addressed to those who are already in Christ Jesus; who have renounced all hope of eternal life from their own works. The calling is to the justified, and to them alone. God leads to the race, and proposes the prize.

15. " Let us then, as many as are adult,* be thus minded ; and if in anything ye be otherwise minded, God shall reveal even this to you. 16. Nevertheless, whereto we have already attained, let us walk by the same rule, let us mind the same thing. 17. Become imitators unitedly† of me, brethren, and regard those who walk so as ye have us for an example."

From the above sentiment it is apparent, that the hope before us is to fill the heart of believers generally. It was not Paul alone that was laid hold on by Christ in order to pursue this end. The exhortation is addressed to every one who is spiritually adult, to keep this hope before him.

For, by "the perfect" of our translation, are meant, "the adult in Christ." Paul had said just before that he did not think himself "perfected." When then he here speaks of himself and others as "perfect," it is in another sense, and one not unfrequently found in the New Testament: Heb. v. The youthful believer is

---

* Τελείοι.　　† Συμμιμηταί μου γίνεσθε.

occupied generally with the truths that concern his own justification and acceptance with God. But when these are clearly seen and firmly held, our position in regard to the coming kingdom, and the need of diligence to obtain the prize, ought deeply to engage our attention.

" As many as are adult." Not all then, even in Philippi, had attained to that stage. The church of that city was indeed one of the most flourishing of that bright day. Yet, even there, there were differences of spiritual knowledge and attainment. The church of Christ is a family, in which there are some of all ages and degrees of grace. But such was the general state of that church, that he could expect to find many of them in a stage of growth to which such an exhortation would be suitable. To these, then, he unveils his heart. He discovers to them the grand motive which actuated himself throughout his christian and apostolic career. All hopes of fulfilling the law in its perfection, and of earning thereby eternal life, were destroyed. Yet that enlightening of his mind did not leave him careless about his works thenceforward, or lead him to think them of no moment in their bearing on eternity. He saw, on the contrary, and would impress on us, the need of incessant and hearty energy, panting for an entrance into the kingdom and glory of our Master. Here lies the great distinction between the present epistle, and the epistles to the Hebrews and to the Corinthians, wherein the same subject is treated. There he uses, indeed, the same motive, but as a *threat* to those believers who were guilty of immorality, or in danger of falling back to the shadows of Judaism. But, on the present occasion, the first resurrection is exhibited as the object of the believer's hope and pursuit. While, then, many think that Christians who receive millennial truth make a great deal too much of it, the passage before us proves, on the contrary, *that they have never yet made it sufficiently prominent.* " Let us, as many as be adult, be thus minded ! "

" He that hath an ear, let him hear what the Spirit saith to the churches."

But, as there were differences of light and grace among the believers of Philippi, lest these should engender strife and division, a word is added to those who saw not the present truth. " And if in any thing ye be otherwise minded, God shall reveal even this to you." The differing from an inspired apostle, of course supposed the dissentients wrong. But if they would apply to the source of light for instruction on those points wherein they differed, either from an apostle, or amongst each other, the truth and the error would be disclosed to them. While, therefore, diversities of view will ever be found among believers, we are hereby taught the way in which they are to be removed, and unity of judgment and of heart to be obtained. " How happens it," say sometimes those who taunt us, " that in spite of your professions of all being instructed by the same Spirit, you are so divided in opinion and at strife among yourselves ? " The answer is very simple; So far as any are taught of the Holy Ghost, they agree . their differences arise from the remains of ignorance and darkness that are blended with the light possessed by each. But behold the remedy for difference provided by God Himself ! It is to ask of Him, with a sincere mind, What is truth ? that it may be held by us : and what is error ? that we may cast it from us. But many cannot afford to know the truth. They would not leave that which it condemns, even if it were shown them to be error. And many trust to argument and discussion, and freedom of speech, as the means of arriving at the truth. But all who have singleness of eye may pray in faith for God's enlightenment of them, on whatever subject they differ ; assured that unity of judgment and of feeling in the church is an object dear to the heart of our Lord : 1 Cor. i, 10.

While seeking th's end, unity is to be maintained still, founded upon agreement in truth already received.

" Whereto we have already attained, let us walk by the same rule." Where this is the case, God's gracious further aid to correct mistakes, and to open the mind to His light, may be confidently expected. " He that hath, to him shall be given, and he shall have abundantly."

The inspired sentiment of the text then stands opposed to the mischievous mistake, which obtained in the church soon after the decease of apostles, that there are *two* rules of life acknowledged by God : one for the perfect—which soon came to mean, the monks and nuns ; and another for the flock in general. But, far from this being true, all, whatever be their measure of attainment, are to walk by the same rule, and to cultivate unity, so that no differences of opinion on subordinate points may effect division among them.

Knowing how much man is a being influenced by example, the Holy Ghost next touches upon the two-fold force of it, exhibiting one class as fit subjects of imitation, the other of reprobation. Paul offers to them, therefore, as living examples of the mode of life fitted to attain the prize, him-self and others like-minded with himself. Thus again a frequent mistake, most pernicious to the well-being of believers, is corrected by the word of truth. Many Christians copy the slothful, covetous, worldly professor, and think themselves safe. " Are they not equal to, or even above, such ? " But that is no security. We are to take as our pattern, the highest style of Christian attainment.

In the early part of the chapter, where the church had to be cautioned against unsound views on the great question of acceptance before God, the snare was *false doctrine*. But we have travelled beyond those limits. A new snare awaited the believers of that day. *False example* might lead them into a mode of life, which would end in their exclusion from the kingdom. And those examples, too, might be found, where there was no denial of the truth, that Jesus was coming to reign. Thus it is also now.

Earthly conduct unsuited to the heavenly calling is a very frequent pit-fall of the enemy in our day.

(18.) " For many are walking, of whom I have told you often, and now tell you even weeping, that they are the enemies of the cross of the Christ ; whose end is destruction, whose god is their belly, and whose glory is in their shame, who mind earthly things."

As the apostle is dissuading Christians from following evil example to their future loss, it would seem to be in the strain of his argument, to exhibit the case of inconsistent believers. And there is much in the nature of their conduct as here painted, which finds an answer in living originals around us. But, as the perseverance of the saints supposes that none of the truly faithful in Christ will finally be lost, this passage must, I suppose, be understood of mere professors of the faith.

Those now aimed at by the apostle were perhaps the parties of whom he spoke, in general terms, in the early part of the epistle, as troubling him by speaking of Christ not with pure intention, for God's glory ; but in order to endanger his life.

They were enemies of Messiah's *cross*. They would not refuse His *kingdom ;* but suffering, as the way to the crown, they rejected wholly. They " mind earthly things." This is increasingly the character of the nominal Christians of the present day. They covet riches ; they seek pleasure ; they study philosophy, and obey its teachings rather than scripture ; they would gladly receive the honours of the world. They are trying to mend the world, and to make themselves a downy nest in it. But the Christian's eye must be on things heavenly. He is to be dead to the things of the world ; alive to those above. Of that, his immersion in water into the name of Christ is a sign.

20. " For our city* is in heaven, from whence† also we are looking for the Lord Jesus Christ as Saviour. 21. Who shall change the body of our humiliation,‡ that it may become conformed to the body of his glory, according to the energy of his ability to subject even all things to himself."

How the twentieth verse stands connected with the subject, is not apparent. It may be designed, as a contrast to the seekers of earthly things just before named. Or it may be joined with verse 17, as completing the description of the adult Christian. " Imitate us ; for our city is in heaven, and there are our hopes and thoughts." The 18th and 19th verses will then come in as a parenthesis. This seems to be the best mode of viewing it.

The Christian, in the above words, is set to look for the return of the Lord Jesus. That is the time of the resurrection of the just, and of the kingdom. Thus the close of the chapter bears out the subject introduced in the centre. Heaven is the place where Jesus now is : and His return is the time of the change of our body, to fit it for immortal blessedness. Thus is the questioned answered—" If our city is on high, how shall we get thither ? " By the return of Jesus the Saviour. " How shall our bodies bear the glory of the heavenly places ? " They shall be changed by His mighty power whose sway all things shall obey.

The body which we now wear is beautifully called, " the body of our humiliation." Ever since sin entered, the body has been subjected to various indignities, aches, infirmities ; humbled by the necessities of infancy and old age, and the changes of the seasons, and at length it becomes the

---

*The word is πολιτευμα, which may translate 'citizenship' ; but I can find no proof of that sense. The word means ' city,' in 2 Macc. xii, 7, and this is, I think, the meaning here. Υπαρχει is best understood too of material existence, as of a city.

† Εν ουρανοις, εξ ου. Grammatically speaking, Jesus is supposed to come forth from the *city*, not from heaven. But the apostle probably means only, ' from heaven.' Εξ ων would have been the correct form.

‡ Το σωμα της ταπεινωσεως ημων.

prey of worms, mingling with the earth. But it is destined to become like the body of Jesus' glory. " Then shall the righteous shine forth as the sun in the kingdom of their Father." Not death, then, but the return of Christ, and the change of our bodies to immortal glory, is the true hope of the believer. Let then the very necessities of our bodies, in place of dragging us down to earth and its shadows, as is the case with the men of the world, teach us to look for that Saviour, whose sudden and promised advent shall instantly remove them !

These are the heavenly hopes, this the divine knowledge of Jesus, which is to supersede in our minds the science of men ; and to teach us to live soberly, righteously, and godly, in this present evil age.

May we move on in obedience to it !

CHAPTER III

THE TWO RESTS

HEB. III, IV.

In these chapters Jesus is compared with Moses, and His superiority to that eminent servant of God is proved. Both were appointed of God; both faithful. But Jesus is superior in nature to Moses; His dispensation is far loftier; and His position in it as much higher, as a son in his own house is above a servant in another's. Then follows our position as believers.

" Whose house are we, if we hold fast to the end the confidence, and the bold profession of hope."*

Moses was conductor and superintendent of a part of the people of God. We are now constituting the spiritual house of God. For there are two houses of God, together making up the one " people of God." While the apostle is about to apply the words of Psalm xcv to us, he still marks the difference of our calling under the gospel from theirs under the law. We are " holy brethren, partakers of the *heavenly* calling." They were partakers of the *earthly*. It is, however, because we belong to the one people of God, and that people consists of the earthly and of the heavenly divisions, that the psalm applies. We take

*Or " of the hope."

our place, under condition of holding firmly unto the end
of the time appointed by God, the objects of faith. The
apostle notices two points required of God; internal confidence in the hope set before us, and external profession
of the same to others: see Rom. x, 8–10.

The word " hope " is to be joined, I believe, to both words :
it is the " confidence " of " hope," and " the bold profession"
of " hope." It was not enough to begin to profess the
Christian hope. It must be retained to the end, even " to
the end of the age." Till then Jesus watches over His
church. " Lo, I am with you all the days unto the end of
the age " : Matt. xxviii, 20.*

He that looks back after putting his hand to the plough,
is not fit for the kingdom of God : Luke ix, 62.

We are now like Israel in Moses' day at the foot of Sinai.
Moses went up into the cloud, after giving them the conditions of the old covenant, and was hidden from their
sight for forty days, till at length they gave up the *hope*
of his return, and instantly fell into idolatry, breaking the
chief stipulation of the old covenant.

The Christian hope is like Israel's at that time. Jesus
having cemented the new covenant with His own blood,
has gone up on high to the presence of God, with a promise,
like Moses, to return. But He has been so long away,
that the glad hope and the profession of the hope of His
return are nearly gone. However, that expectation which
first characterized the Christian, is still to be ·held, still
to be professed.

" Wherefore, (as saith the Holy Spirit—' To-day if ye will
hear his voice, harden not your hearts as in the provocation,
during the day of the temptation† in the wilderness, where‡ your
fathers tempted me, proved me, and saw my works forty years.
Therefore I was grieved with that generation, and said, —They
are always erring in heart, but they know not my ways. So I
sware in my wrath, They shall not enter into my rest.') "

*See Greek.   †Or " of temptation."   ‡Or " when."

The apostle enforces the duty of holding fast, by the citation of a portion of the xcvth Psalm. He speaks of it as uttered by the Holy Ghost, to give the greater solemnity to the words. It was written indeed by David, but it was inspired of God. The reach and application of the sentiment expressed was beyond David's comprehension ; but not beyond His, who searches the deep things of God.

The passage contains a call to listen, and not to be like the fathers, whose sins and consequent punishment are then recounted.

They tempted God. The tempting God means the trying experiments with Him ; putting Him to the proof by some difficulty presented, which it is supposed He cannot or will not solve.* So Jesus was tempted, when the difficulty about paying tribute, which they thought unanswerable, was put to Him. Thus they tempted the Lord at Rephidim, when they thought He could not give them water to drink. The place took afterwards the name of Massah, ("Temptation") from the tempting of God which there took place : Ex. xvii, 7.

His many miracles drew not forth their hearts to love, to fear, or to obey, though repeated for forty years. Their errors were not mistakes of the understanding, but rebellion of the heart. It was perpetual transgression *there*, though it did not always exhibit itself to the eye of man. Though they were brought so close to God, and had such experience of His character, manifested in startling acts of judgment and of mercy, they understood not His ways. At length then their former offences, for a time passed by, are at Kadesh reckoned up against them, and the oath of God, that they should not enter the land, went forth. That oath, once uttered, all hope of change on God's part was

*So Joan of Arc was tempted, when professing to have a message to the King of France, a courtier took his place and robes, and the king stood among his nobles, to test her whether she would discover the cheat.

precluded, and they did not even attempt to obtain the reversal of it.

12. "Take heed, brethren, lest there be in any of you an evil heart of unbelief in departing from the living God."

This verse stands connected with verse 7, the intermediate quotation being a parenthesis "Wherefore (as the Holy Ghost saith, &c.) take heed."

Strong as the words of the passage are, they are an address to BELIEVERS. This the apostle would have us clearly perceive. "Lest there be *in any of you* an evil heart of unbelief." "Exhort one another *lest any of you* be hardened through the deceitfulness of sin." "Let *us* therefore fear, lest . . . . . *any of you* should seem to come short." "Take heed, *brethren*." You are, like Israel, redeemed out of Egypt. You, as they were, have been delivered by the blood of the Lamb. You have made profession of faith in Jesus. Faith dwells in you. But beware ! The old man is not wholly rooted out. Unbelief in part exists, though it may lie hid. It needs to be kept under. And all unbelief leads our hearts away from the God of life, and from His words of life.

If there be unbelief in the heart, it will somehow or other manifest itself in the conduct, in departure from God. Christ is here called, as I suppose, "the living God "* He is seen to be "the Resurrection and Life," by His rising from the dead. The revolters from Moses sought to make another captain, and to go back to Egypt. But to leave the apostle of our calling now, is to revolt from the Prince of Life.

13. "But exhort one another each day, while it is called 'to-day,' lest any of you be hardened by the deceitfulness of sin."

*God is called by this title four times in the epistle : iii, 12 ; ix, 14 ; x, 31 ; xii, 22.

We are here instructed to use means against the danger
of falling away. The means are continual exhortation :
the stirring up one another to reverence and obey God's
word. Means are nothing without God ; but God works
by blessing means.

As the voice of temptation is often repeated, so is the
voice of exhortation to be frequently repeated also. As
Caleb and Joshua lifted up their voices against the evil
spies, and the unbelieving people, so should we seek to
engage the Lord's people to desire His promises, and to
tread in the steps of obedience that lead to their attainment.
Exhortation is but for a time. It is to be exerted " while
it is called to-day." The time of temptation and the
season when the means of resisting it are needed, will soon
be over.

" While it is called to-day." It is the privilege of God
to appoint " times and seasons." " Are there not twelve
hours in the day ? " He measures out its length. God's
words imply *things*. When He testifies the end of this age,
when He proclaims that the new day is come, He will also
change the features of the time. The darkness of this
present evil age will depart, and the glory of the day which
the Lord hath made, and in which His people shall rejoice,
will set in. " While it is called to-day," Satan is the prince
of the world, the flesh is dying and corrupt, and the stream
of the world runs counter to the Spirit of God. But faith
sees " the day approaching " which will change all this
cloud and storm into glory and joy.

Those who do not listen to the word of the Lord, and to
the right exhortation, grow hardened through the deceitfulness of sin. The most lowly reverence and prompt
obedience become a sinner listening to the Word of God.
Yet many resist its calls, on some one point or other. And
with each resistance of truth, hardness grows on the soul.
The spirit deadens to the apprehension of the promises,

and grows careless at the threats of God. Sin deceives even the believer whenever it gains an entrance. It is a creeping cancer slowly spreading. It is a winter frost, by degrees hardening the pool, till it can bear unbroken the laden waggon.

14. "For we have become associates* of the Christ, if we hold firmly to the end the beginning of our full conviction." (faith.)†

The authorized version gives the commencing words a different rendering, but one not easy of comprehension. The apostle, I suppose, had in his eye his former quotation of the xlvth Psalm, in which the same word occurs. "But unto the Son he saith, Thy throne O God, is for ever and ever, a sceptre of righteousness is the sceptre of thy kingdom. Thou lovedst righteousness and hatedst iniquity, wherefore, O God, thy God anointed thee with the oil of gladness above thy *fellows.*" μετοχους: 1, 8, 9. Paul therefore refers back to this. The xivth Psalm gives us the advent of the Messiah in the glory of His kingdom. He is God—"Thy throne O *God*" He is man—"Above thy *fellows.*" *God* has no *fellow-men.* We are there shown the height of glory reserved as the prize of our heavenly calling. It is to be "associates" or "*fellows*" "of the Messiah" in His kingdom. The tribes of Israel are to be Messiah's *subjects,* we His *household* and *joint heirs.* Faith has put us in the way of realizing that height of glory. It will be ours, *if* we hold fast to the end our confident expectation of the kingdom of Messiah and His glory. For those who diligently seek Him, God has great rewards in store. But believers who harden themselves against His word, though they may finally enter eternal life, will be cut off from that scene of bliss.

* Μετοχοι.

† Before, (ver. 6) it was παρρησια ; now the writer uses another word—υποστασις.

The verse before us much resembles verse 6 above. There we were declared to be Messiah's house, *if* we continued steadfast. Both promises are conditional. We are now engaged, not about the question of *eternal life*, which is a free gift ; but about the *kingdom*, which is a reward according to works, and may be lost by disobedience.

The present verse seems chiefly connected, not with the verse immediately preceding it, but with the twelfth. " Take heed, lest by unbelief you depart from the living God. For your position in the Kingdom of Glory will be that of Messiah's associates, if you hold fast."

Let a sense, then, of the lofty dignity prepared for the victor, keep us from disobedience !

15. " While it is said, ' To-day, if ye will hear his voice, harden not your hearts, as in the provocation.' "

As long as God calls to us to listen, so long we must obey. As long as He pleases to extend the day of trial to ourselves and others, so long we are to second His call by cheering on our fellows to obtain the prize, against whatever foes arise to rob us of the crown. " Hold fast that which thou hast ; that none take thy crown." " Look to yourselves, that we lose not the things that we have wrought, but that we receive a full reward."

16. " For who, after having heard, provoked ? Why, was it not all that came out of Egypt by Moses ?

17. And with whom was he grieved forty years ? Was it not with them that sinned, whose carcases fell in the wilderness ?

18. And to whom sware he that they should not enter into his rest, but to those that disobeyed ? "*

These verses should be read as questions throughout ; as the sense requires, and as, I believe, all modern critics are agreed.

* Απειθησασι. Our translation neglects the important difference between απιστια, and απειθεω.

The apostle is commenting on the words of the psalm quoted above. Israel heard God's voice at Sinai, yet hardened their hearts. The mount of thunder should have impressed the fear of Jehovah on their souls for ever. But, in a little while, all dread was gone. In that little word— "Who?" lies the force of the whole passage. Who *provoked?* Yes, that is the question! In the answer to it lies the power of the application to ourselves. It was not the Jebusite, or the Amorite, but *the redeemed by blood that did so!*

Was Israel provoking, and perverse, perpetually? Now rises the cry—"We are dying of hunger!" Now—"We perish by thirst!" Now—"Give us flesh to eat!" Now — "Make us gods to go before us!" Yes, it was stubborn and aggravating indeed; *but the Church of Christ has been no better.*

The Holy Spirit would press on our attention the wide spread of sin. All the congregation, save Caleb and Joshua, were convicted of trespass, and cut off in the wilderness. Here lies the remedy for a subtle plea of unbelief. Sin deceives us with the thought, that if offenders be very numerous, if all the Christians around us are guilty of disobedience, we may march on with them undismayed. So thought Israel. They were confident in numbers. The whole assembly rose against Caleb and Joshua. But Jehovah hesitated not, because the trespassers were a multitude. He smote by units or by thousands, according to the numbers of the sinners.

They provoked God. Learn, then, that God has feelings as truly as man. The breach of His commands, the refusal to credit Him, rouse His displeasure, in the case of the saint as truly as in the case of the sinner. Believer, grieve not the Holy Spirit! Provoke not the living God!

When a believer marries an unbeliever, contrary to His command, is not God provoked? When a saint seeks to be rich in this world, contrary to the Lord's precept, is he not likely to be cut off from the kingdom ?

17. But the Lord was not only provoked. He manifested His displeasure by corresponding actions. Though ransomed out of Egypt, yet they became carcases in the wilderness. The people of God died under His frown of anger. He shewed them mercies, but they requited Him with sins, till He would endure it no longer. Space for repentance was no longer given. They fell, without obtaining the hope set before them.

18. 19. At length the oath of God, never to be retracted, was launched against them. They were excluded, *on grounds not peculiar to them, but capable of applying as truly to God's people now.* They should not enter, because of unbelief, and its product, disobedience. It was *partial* unbelief. They believed in the first miracles of Moses. They believed, as was manifested in marking their doors with the blood of the Lamb. They had faith, so far as to cross the Red Sea, when commanded : Heb. xi, 28, 29. But partial unbelief led to frequent acts of disobedience, till the door of promise was shut against them altogether. *This, therefore completes the application of the passage to the saints of the Church of Christ.* How necessary for us to try every doctrine that we hear by Scripture, lest we habitually receive the false, and deny the true !

Unbelief, in its fullness, shuts out from *eternal life :* Acts xiii, 46. But partial unbelief, and its accompanying evil conduct, may at length exclude from *the rest of God.*

IV. 1. " Let us therefore fear, lest a promise being left of entering into his rest any of you should think he has come too late for it."*

The promise of rest indirectly made in the Psalm, is

*See Greek.
† Καταλειπομενης. Afterwards, v, 9. απολειπεται.

still in force. The word "left"† means the opposite to being "fulfilled."

Believers are to fear, lest this promise should be unfulfilled towards themselves. "*Any one of you* should think he has come too late for it." The apostle is not treating of the failure of the Gentiles as a body, but of loss to the individual Christian. The promise, which before referred to them, is now transmitted to you and your time. As *they* lost its efficacy for themselves, so may *you*. Be diligent then, that this sad result be not yours.

"A promise." The same great object of hope and of earnest effort, is assumed, not only throughout this epistle, but throughout the New Testament: Eph. iv, 4. In this epistle it is called by various names, "the good news," "the promise," "the rest," "the sabbatism," "the kingdom."

If we translate as in the received version, "*seem* to come short of it," there is involved, I believe, a reference to the taking and the leaving spoken of by our Lord. The day is coming, when Jesus will suddenly take to himself the watchful saint, leaving behind the careless one.

But the Greek word translated "to come short," means also to come too late. The allusion is to a race, or to a feast. The unready virgins came, but at length too late for the supper, and they are shut out: Matt. xxv.

Here again, the same strong exhortation of the Spirit presses on us. It is addressed to *saints*. It warns them not to be secure ; but to remember, that God will decide whether we shall enter His rest or not, according to our conduct. The disobedient saint will lose the future reality, as surely as Israel lost the past type. For we have to do with the same God, who after having made them His people, and sustained them by mercies, justly demanded of them a life of obedience. The entrance to the rest is still open, and dependent on our behaviour. If the Lord's oath of exclusion embrace us as well as them, we shall certainly be shut out of that future scene of reward.

2. "For to us has good news been brought* as well as to them; but the word of the report† profited them not, not being mixed with faith in them that heard it."

The Greek word is here taken in its future general sense of "good news." The glad tidings of the rest belongs as truly to us as to them. Here its application to us is directly asserted. The promise, not having received-its accomplishment in Moses' day, knocks at our doors now for admittance.

The good news is the good news of Messiah's millennial kingdom. That was the strain taken up by Jesus and by His servant John, as soon as the new dispensation commenced. "And Jesus went about all Galilee teaching in their synagogues, and preaching *the gospel* OF THE KINGDOM, and healing all manner of sickness and all manner of disease among the people " · Matt. iv, 23; ix, 35. "And this *gospel* OF THE KINGDOM shall be preached in all the habitable earth for a witness unto all nations; and then shall the end come " : Matt. xxiv, 14.

Our translation, by rendering the next expression—" the word *preached*"—has caused the general reader to lose the allusion intended by the apostle. There is, I doubt not, a reference to the history of Israel just before they were excluded by oath. God promised them by Moses, " a land flowing with milk and honey " : Exod. iii, 8, 17. At first, on seeing the miracles of their leader, they believed. But, as they drew near the land, doubt crept in. They desired that some might be sent to search the country. Their request was complied with. Twelve spies were commissioned to enter it. At their return they brought back

---

* Εσμεν ευηγγελισμενοι.

† Ο λογος της ακοης.

the report.* " And they told him and said, we came unto the land whither thou sentest us, and surely it floweth with milk and honey ; and this is the fruit of it." But " *the word of the report* did not profit them." " They despised the pleasant land ; they *believed not his word,* but murmured in their tents, and *hearkened not unto the voice of the Lord. Therefore he lifted up his hand against them,* [he swore] *to overthrow them in the wilderness* " : Psa. cvi, 24–26.

As God spoke of His rest as future, He was still engaged in work : but not that of creation, spoken of in Gen. ii.

The promise, then, was not fulfilled to them ; not through any failure of power, or of truth in God ; but owing to their own fault. The report was not " mixed with faith in them that heard it." The food was good, but it was not digested. No food sustains the body that is not mixed with gastric juice. God's power to fulfil His word was seen in bringing in the younger portion of the congregation under Joshua.

No report will profit, unless we believe it. None will grow rich by the gold in Australia, unless he believes that it is to be had there, and acts upon it.

" For we who have believed are entering into the rest, as he said,—' So I sware in my wrath, they shall not enter into my rest : ' although the works from the foundation of the world were finished. 4. For he spake in a certain place concerning the seventh day thus, ' And God rested on the seventh day from all his works.' 5. And in this place again, ' They shall not enter into my rest.' "

The argument which follows is designed to afford an answer to the question—" What is the rest intended ? " Paul shews that it is a *future one.* This idea, however, is

*Numb. xiii, 32 ; xiv, 37. In regard to the future kingdom, the twelve apostles are the new spies. As the ancient ones were forty days searching the land, so, to the apostles for forty days Jesus was " speaking of the things pertaining to *the kingdom of God :* " Acts i, 3. And, as the spies brought back some of the fruit with them as a specimen, so the twelve bore with them to the churches, the gifts of the Holy Ghost, as specimens of the powers of the coming age.

quite obscured in our translation, by the rendering " do enter," and the omission of the article before " rest."

We, as believers, are, like Israel, moving on toward the rest.

1. It should be rendered—" The works from the foundation of the world had taken place." The order of the Greek shows this—" We are entering into the rest," for it is future, though Scripture speaks of one past.

Each day brings us nearer to the time and the place of the future rest. As unbelief excluded from the rest, so faith sets us on our way towards it. It is to us, as believers, that the race for the prize is set open. No unbeliever can enter in. He who has not the kingdom within, can never see the kingdom without.

By "*the* rest " is meant, that proclaimed in the psalm above cited. To make this clear, the verse that speaks of rest is then quoted afresh.

But the assertion of the *futurity* of the rest promised in the psalm, is instantly checked by the admission of a *past* rest. " Although the works from the foundation of the world *were finished*." That is, ' I grant, that the Scripture speaks elsewhere of God's work being completed ; and, as the consequence, of His rest having been taken, as soon as creation was finished. Finished work implies rest ; and the Scripture uses the very term " rest " of God's position on the seventh day.* But it also as clearly affirms a *future* rest in the psalm I have quoted. " They *shall* not enter into my rest.'—It was a *new* work of God that then was going on, from which He purposed to rest, and into which others were to have entrance ; with God enjoying the rest.

It is necessary then, in order to understand this passage, to admit two rests of God : a *past* one, fulfilled on the

* Καταπαυσις κατεπαυσεν. But the words in the Hebrew are not alike. This difference is taken up afterwards.

seventh day: a *future* one, supposed in the xcvth Psalm.* The abruptness of the argument, however, renders it difficult to trace its course.

Two senses may be given to the words, " my rest." The expression may mean—

1. " The *rest* which I *enjoy*." (Subjective.)

2. " The rest which I *provide*." (Objective.)

Now the passages quoted are types of each of these two senses. (1) That from Genesis—" And God rested on the seventh day "—speaks of the rest which He Himself *enjoyed*. (2.) But the future rest of the Psalm, from which unbelievers are to be excluded, is as clearly, the rest which God has *provided;* to be enjoyed by others as well as partaken of by Himself. In this sense, the words " mv supper " are taken in the parable of our Lord: Luke xiv, 24. In this sense, too, it agrees with the remarkable expression in Romans, which is the key to the Epistle—" the righteousness of God." In the same sense Moses uses it of the promise to Israel: " Ye are not as yet come to *the rest* and to the inheritance, *which the Lord your God giveth you* ": Deut. xii, 9.

Now " the rest of God " applies to *us* in both these senses. Each has its spiritual antitype. There is a *past* rest of God, into which *we have already entered* by faith; just because there is a past work of God in which He is now resting. For Jesus, during His life, wrought out a righteousness for us, and endured the curse of the law in death. That work of His was complete in resurrection. In that completed work the whole Godhead already *rests*, with a greater complacency than in the finished work of the seventh day. " When God speaks of His rest, of course He means not the long-finished works, and the long-past rest of creation and the seventh

---

*Hence Stuart and others who wish to throw down the adversative meaning of Καιτοι, by rendering it 'namely,' have missed the sense of the passage.

day : yet the future rest is like it, as the like expression shows."

The first rest of God in creation was broken by unrighteousness entering. Then came in the sentence of death, and the work was blighted and marred. In order to its recovery, then, there is a twofold work, and a twofold rest. Righteousness was first to be wrought, to undo the sin brought in. That has been completed ; and God rests in the work thus far accomplished. But the sentence of travail and death, as the issue of unrighteousness, abides still : and that has yet to be removed, ere the full rest of God can come in. This is the *future* rest of the psalm to which we are invited ; God rejoicing in His works anew. Of that the seventh day was a type. And the Lord's day is the day of present rest, on which we celebrate the work of Christ completed.

God rested on the seventh day from *all* His works. The works then of which the psalm makes mention—" They proved me and saw *my works*," are of another class, than those of the creation. Sin destroyed God's former rest in creation. He began then to *work* anew, to bring in a better *rest*. But the disobedient perceived not the ways of the Lord, and sympathized neither in His work, nor in His rest. Wherefore the Lord was angry with " that *generation*." But does " that generation " mean only those who died in the wilderness ? By no means. As the *day* abides in which God is showing His ways, and displaying His works ; and as the *rest* still is held out, so the *generation* abides still. Jesus assures us, that it will not be purged out, till the awful judgments of the *day* of the Lord sweep it from the face of the earth. " Verily I say unto you, this *generation* will not pass away, till all these things be fulfilled " · Matt. xxiv, 34. Let not us then be found amidst the unintelligent and disobedient generation !

6. " Since, then, it remaineth that some should enter into it and they to whom the glad tidings were first proclaimed entered not in through disobedience, he again limiteth a certain day."*

The Israelites, to whom the promise of God's rest was first announced, lost it through disobedience. But God's word cannot return to him in vain. Some, therefore, must enter. As they who were disobedient were excluded, the class which is to enter, is hinted at as the opposite to the unruly and disobedient.

7. " Saying by David, ' To-day,' after so long a time, as it has been before said† ' To-day if ye will hear his voice, harden not your hearts.' 8. For if Joshua had given them rest, he would not speak of another day after these things."

This is a carrying out of the proof, that the rest meant by the Holy Spirit has not been fulfilled. It is true, that on the death of Moses, Joshua led in the spared ones of Israel into the land. It is true that God is said to have given him rest. " And He gave them *rest* round about, according to all that He sware unto their fathers " : Josh. xxi, 44. " And now the Lord hath given *rest* unto your brethren, as He promised them " : Josh. xxii, 4. Yet still that rest was not the one intended by God in the psalm. For if it had been enjoyed, it would not so long after have been spoken of as an object still to be striven for.

So again it is true, that God is said to have given to David and to Solomon " rest." (1) To David—" And it came to pass, when the king sat in his house, and the Lord had given him *rest* from all his enemies " : 2 Sam. vii, 1. (2) To Solomon ("the Peaceful ") it was peculiarly promised. " Behold a son shall be born to thee (David) who shall be a *man of rest ;* and I will give him *rest* from all his enemies round about " : 1 Chron. xxii, 9.

But, as God spoke by David of the rest as still future, it is evident, that even David's day of prosperity, and Israel's

* Απειθεια.

† Προειρηται, the preferable reading.

enjoyment of political rest in the promised land under himself and his son, was not the rest designed of God. *God is not said to have rested.*

Four hundred years after Joshua had led Israel into the land, the day of temptation and of God's call to listen lest the rest should be lost, was still running on. Even in David's time, the call to hearken "to-day" was still in force. If Joshua's rest of thirty or forty years were the one indicated, the promise would not have been spoken of in David's reign as unfulfilled.

"Another day." The six days of creation were natural days : so was the seventh. But "the *day* of temptation" in the wilderness was forty years. Hence "day" is taken in a new sense. God's calling the period from Joshua or from Moses till the present time by the name of "to-day," gives a further extension to the term. The day of rest, which is to follow on this, will also be an extended day "Beloved, be not ignorant of this one thing, that one day is with the Lord as a thousand years, and a thousand years as one day." The present day of labour, of suffering to the saints, and of trial to the world, has its limit already defined in the mind of God. The day of rest, which is to follow it, has its limit also. God's rest is to be the period of a "day." If Joshua's had been the day of rest, he would not have spoken of "another *day*." The next verse takes up and expands this idea.

9. "There remaineth therefore the keeping of a sabbath-rest for the people of God."

This is the issue of the argument. The rest promised in the xcvth Psalm is yet unfulfilled. It is to be the object of the Christian's desire and pursuit.

To-day is the day of labour, of sorrow from the world, and of God's trial of His people. *To-morrow* then is the day of rest and of reward. Hold out through the hours of "to-day," and a long to-morrow will make you amends.

The word used to describe " the rest " is changed.* The apostle coins a word to express the " sabbath-rest " that is to come.

Thus it is intimated to us, that though God's rest on the seventh day from the work of creation was not the rest intended in the psalm, it was yet a type of it. The millennial rest will be, as the apostle seems to hint, in the seventh thousand year of the world's history. Then the work of the six previous days will cease, and God will rejoice with His people. As a foreshadowing of God's plan in regard to this, the law signalized the seventh day, the seventh week, the seventh month, the seventh year, and the seven times seventh year, by ordinances prefiguring the sabbath yet to be kept. In harmony with this, the apostle has twice named " the seventh day," as the period of God's creation-rest.

And though the rest to which Joshua introduced the remnant of Israel was not the true rest of God, yet it was a type of it. So was the glorious day of the kingdom under Solomon, the Son of David, " the man of rest." All lend their aid to typify the future sabbatism. The coming rest will embrace creation, as did that of the first seventh day. It will especially embrace Israel, and the land of promise. It will be the result of a victory over the foes of God, as was Joshua's rest.

This period of joy is awaiting " the people of God." But that people, as the epistle testifies, is *twofold ;* those of the earthly calling, and those of the heavenly. In ch. xi, the worthies of the old Testament are set before us as the children of faith, justified thereby, and so possessors of the rest provided by God in the righteousness of another. They are seen also as the obedient ones, and therefore ready to enter with us into the promised rest, whenever the time of

---

*It is no longer καταπαυσις, but σαββατισμος. So in the Hebrew of Gen. ii, 2, the word is not מנוחתי as in the Psalm, but וישבת.

God's appointment · shall have come. The same good tidings have been laid before both ; the same sabbath repose is prepared for both.*

But this view confirms the conclusion, that the sabbath-rest here spoken of is the millennial. We are directed in the present passage to *strive for* the rest of God. And Paul tells us, that his earnest *effort* was directed to obtain part in the resurrection *from among the dead* ; that is, the millennial first resurrection. Peter again urges on the saints, to use all diligence, that so the abundant *entrance into the Kingdom* of Christ might be granted them : 2 Pet. i, 5–10. Here striving for *entrance into the rest* spoken of by Paul in the Hebrews answers to Peter's striving to obtain the *entrance into the Kingdom*. Now as the Holy Ghost assures us, that we are " called ᵗn *one hope of our calling*," the two expressions are but different views of the same thing. And Paul's striving for the select resurrection as " *the prize of our high calling*," on the same principle proves the same conclusion. Finally, Jesus urges His hearers to take heed, lest they should be shut out from the kingdom of God, in which the patriarchs and the believing of the Gentiles would be united, while unbelievers and the dis-obedient would be cast out.

10. " For he that entered into his rest, he also hath rested from his own works as God did from his."

This is, I believe, spoken primarily of Christ.

The former verse exhibited the sabbath as it stands related to the *future* rest of God. But this verse notices that a *present* sabbath or rest is already enjoyed by the believer. This rest is entered upon by faith at once. Hence, as the faith of all whom the apostle was addressing had already

*Not that this supposes, that saints of the Law will occupy the same position and dignity in that day, that will be held by the church.

begun, the entrance into it is spoken of as past. " He that *has entered* into his rest."

Every believer rightly instructed has already, in this sense, entered into God's rest. He has ceased from all attempts to obtain righteousness by his own works. He beholds that great object completely fulfilled for him in the righteousness of God, which Jesus finished. He contemplates that work with peace and complacency, as God did His works of creation when they came from His hand perfect. " *His own* works," he sees, even the very best are " dead works," of which he has need to repent, and from which his conscience must be cleansed, ere he can truly serve the living God : Heb. vi, 1 ; ix, 14. But he is now to be diligent, in the power of the life of God, to do the works of God. The hope of the future *rest of God* can only be laid on the foundation of the completed *righteousness of God*.

The law could not give true rest, for it could not give righteousness. The rest of the Old Testament " Jesus " (*i.e.* Joshua), must needs be imperfect : for it was founded on his own and Israel's obedience. But the New Testament " Jesus " is leading His people into rest, on the ground of a perfect righteousness.

Israel rejects the rest offered in the righteousness of Christ. It sought, and seeks still, to maintain its own righteousness. And hence the children of the kingdom will be cast into outer darkness, while believing Gentiles will come from the east and west, and sit down in the kingdom of God. For without a better righteousness than the Pharisees, there shall be no permission to enter the future kingdom of God.

11. " Let us therefore earnestly endeavour to enter into that other rest, lest any fall after the same example of disobedience."

The two rests are contrasted in this verse, and in the preceding. The one is already enjoyed ; the other is to be the object of our earnest effort to attain. The first is requisite in order to labour for the second. Those possessed of the rest in God's righteousness are to press towards the future rest, as the very design of God in calling them to the first.

A beautiful comment on these verses is furnished by Paul's Epistle to the Philippians, chap. iii, which has been already considered. There he first describes his confidence as a Jew in his own merits and works; but afterwards his rejection of them all, in favour of the righteousness which is obtained from God by faith. But then, he adds, that he set out with eager effort to attain, if possible, an entrance into the second rest of the kingdom, at the resurrection of the just.

Thus the Christian's position is a paradox. He is resting and he is labouring. He is resting, while it is called to-day, from all toil to procure himself a righteousness. It is his already by faith. He is resting in this; for God is resting in it also. His present rest of soul is Jesus' promise; " Come unto me all ye that labour and are heavy laden, and I will give you *rest* " : Matt. xi, 28.

But he is working also, " while it is called to-day," for the future rest; for God is working too, to bring in a new and complete rest. And God is calling him, as the racer, to run for the crown; as the wrestler, to strive for the prize.

He is to rest from toil to-morrow; then to find the peace of God *without*, which now he enjoys only *within*. Of Messiah's day to come it is said, " *his rest* shall be glory " : Isa. xi. But now it is written, " In the world ye shall have *tribulation* " · John xvi, 33. " We must through *much tribulation* enter the kingdom of God " : Acts xiv.

12. " For the word of God is living,* and powerful, and sharper than any two-edged sword, and reaching even to the dividing of soul and spirit, of the joints and marrow, and judges the thoughts and intents of the heart. 13. Nor is there any creature hid before it, but all things are naked and open to the eyes of him, to whom our account (is to be given.")

* Ζων.

Thus does the Holy Spirit meet and rebuke that low and unbelieving view which the human mind naturally takes of the Word of God. It is ever apt to think : ' Such and such portions are obsolete, they can have no manner of bearing upon us ! '

In the present instance we are ready to suppose that the psalm refers only to events long past, in which we have no concern. But Paul vindicates the Word of God. No : its reach extends far beyond the day of Moses, of Joshua, or David. It is not dead and out of date. No : it applies with full force still to us of the present day. The word of the living God is an image of Himself. It is living too.

It is mighty in its promises to the believer, transforming, purifying him. It is mighty also to cut and wound by its threats, where resisted and despised.

As God beholds the heart, so His word, a mirror of His intelligence, arraigns the thoughts of man ; no less than his deeds. " They always err in *heart*." " Harden not your *hearts*."

Some of the Hebrews might be even now pondering the step of apostasy. Here is a salutary warning, Such a thought was known to God, rebuked by His word even now, and to be punished hereafter, unless repented of.

Thus the question of the rest of God ends with an appeal to His word, as the basis of our account before God as our Judge. May we solemnly weigh its appeal !

CHAPTER IV

THE TWO OATHS

HEB. v, 11 ; vi.

IN an earlier portion of the epistle to the Hebrews, Paul had recommended Jesus to our notice as the high priest, no less than the apostle of our profession. He broke off from this topic to treat of Jesus' office as compared with Moses', and of the superior rest into which he is leading the partakers of the better calling. At iv, 14, he again resumes the subject of Jesus' high priesthood, in order to manifest its superiority to that of Aaron ; presenting it in three different points of view.

1. He unfolds the general nature of priesthood.

2. The priest should be of sympathetic nature.

3. He ought not to be self-appointed.

In treating of these things as discovered in our Lord, he offers the three subjects in an inverted order.

3. Jesus was appointed by God ; as is proved by two of the psalms.

2. He is of a sympathizing character.

1. He is entitled by God " High Priest after the order of Melchisedec."

Hereupon the apostle digresses into the long parenthesis which we now propose to consider. He reverts not again to the subject of Jesus' priesthood, till he has brought round the matter to the high priesthood of Melchisedec again.

It is evident, therefore, that much turns upon our rightly viewing that portion of Old Testament history.

11. "Concerning whom (Melchisedec) we have many things to say, and difficult of explanation, seeing ye are become* dull of hearing."

The apostle felt a difficulty in bringing before them this topic, as it involved deeper knowledge of the preceding truths of God, than they were at present in possession of. Yet the obstacles lay more in the unpreparedness of the persons, than in the intrinsic difficulties of the subject itself. Difficulty should rather rouse interest, than settle us down into sloth. The greater the impediments to enter into a truth, the greater our joy and admiration of it when mastered. What patience does the natural philosopher discover in investigating the objects and laws of natural science ! What eager audiences does the narrator of discoveries in astronomy, phrenology, and chemistry find ? Is it only in the things of God that his people are slow to put forth effort ? and unwilling to believe that anything more can be learned from his word than has already been known by them ?

That which gave the apostle his chief pain in addressing them was, that they had " *become* dull of hearing." Once they were all alive to listen ; greeted each added truth with joy, as a new lump of golden ore. Now that zeal had passed. Their attention flagged ; with listlessness they regarded the word of God ; as that which could no longer afford them anything new or interesting.

12. " For when in consideration of the time, ye ought to be teachers, ye have again need that one should teach you* the first principles ('the elements of the beginning of the oracles,' literally), of the oracles of God : and are become such as have need of milk

* Γεγονατε.

and not of solid food. 13. For every one that partaketh of milk is unskilful in the word of righteousness : for he is a babe. 14. But solid food belongs to adults ; who have by reason of use their senses exercised to distinguish good and evil."

Not ordination, but knowledge and love of gospel truths was of old the great moral qualification for teaching. It was expected that Christians should grow in knowledge as they advanced in years, and be able to impart to others the truths they had learned. All might not be able to speak in public ; but all, after they had long learned, ought to be fit to communicate truth in private. But instead of being able to impart truth to others, the Hebrew Christians needed themselves to be instructed afresh, in principles which lay at the root of the Christian faith. They required to have impressed on them truths relating to their own acceptance before God.

The Scriptures of the Old and New Covenants are " the oracles of God." The heathen had some oracles, which were consulted by the kings and nobles adjacent to them, at considerable expense. Their answers were often so ambiguous, as to be capable of two opposite meanings ; or else they were so dark, as to be incapable of being understood. Not so *our* " oracles." They relate God's views of the past ; they teach present duty ; they disclose the future with surprising clearness.

The first truths of Christianity Paul calls by the name of milk. Considered in relation to the time during which they had professed Christ, they were adults ; but they were still unable to digest anything stronger than milk. With adult age should come the food of adults. But it was not so with them.

Again the rebuke is administered, that *it was not so at first."* " I remember the time when it was otherwise ; and you sought for and fed upon the deeper truths of Christ.

*I take τινα, not as agreeing with στοιχεια. but as the inefinite pronoun before the verb διδασκειν.

How melancholy to find the adult that once lived on solids, returning again to the weak liquids suited to infancy ! " But this was in fulfilment of that word—" He that hath, to him shall be given, and he shall have abundantly ; *but he that hath not, from him shall be taken even that which he seemeth to have.*" Neglected truths slip from both the heart and the memory.

What a rebuke does this passage administer to the Christians of our day ! They are ever dwelling only on the first principles of the gospel. The question of their own salvation is the only theme almost that seems to keep up its interest. Most will have it so. " We only want just to get to heaven, that is enough for us ! "

But against those who are lingering ever about these first elements of repentance and faith, a wide field of beauty and instruction is ever closed. They are " unskilful in the word of righteousness." But what is meant by that phrase— " the word of righteousness ? " I take it to signify, " the Old Testament," in opposition to " the principles of the doctrine of Christ " which are mentioned soon after. The Old Testament or its conditions of salvation are called, " the law of righteousness " : Rom. ix, 31. Righteousness was its demand, the justice of God was the attribute it was intended mainly to disclose. In opposition thereto the gospel utterances are called " *the word of his grace* " : Acts xx, 32 ; " the word of reconciliation " : 2 Cor. v, 19 ; " the word of this salvation " : Acts xiii, 26. The Holy Ghost is called " the Spirit of *grace*," Heb. x, 29, and the throne which God now occupies is called " the throne of *grace* " · Heb. iv, 16.

John the Baptist, too, as coming in the Old Testament spirit is said by our Lord to have come " in the way of righteousness " · Matt. xxi, 32. For John came " in the spirit and power of Elias," standing aloof from sinners after the example of that prophet of the old covenant. See also in further proof, Psa. cxix, 123, 138, 172 ; Prov. viii, 8, 20.

The meaning then of the sentiment will be, that those in the lukewarm state here supposed, are ignorant of the meaning of the Old Testament as typifying Christ and the things to come. This idea is fully in harmony with what precedes. It is when the apostle was about to expound how Old Testament history typically represented the glory of Christ, that he utters the rebuke before us. It is quite evident, that he who scarcely comprehends and receives the main offices of Christ as set forth in the plain words of the New Testament, will not perceive him as presented under the veil of type in the Old.

Herein again then, the infirmity of our present Christianity is seen. The first and literal sense of either volume is milk ; the second or more hidden sense is solid food. It demands more *faith* in the hearer as well as more knowledge in the teacher. To take an instance. The history of Rebecca brought to Isaac contains lessons to the saints on the importance of prayer and taking counsel of God in all things, specially in the matter of marriage. These truths lie on the surface. But another far deeper and New Testament series of truths is discovered therein, when we see it a history typical of the church brought to Christ by the Holy Spirit. It is chiefly in its typical aspect that the Old Testament affects us. The history of Abraham's wives and sons (Gal. iv.) would apply to us in the apostle's argument only when taken spiritually.

It greatly confirms the view above given to notice where the rebuke of the apostle comes in. He had treated of two of the qualifications of the high priest, ere he begins his reproof. But he has to speak of the appointment of Christ as Priest " after the order of *Melchisedec*." But Melchisedec was an Old Testament person, and the application of his history to the elucidation of Messiah's position required " *interpretation*." That is, it requires us to receive it as *typical*. His names, the circumstances under which Abraham met him, the words he spoke, the title of God

which he employs, all are typical ; that is, prophetic of
" the age to come."

To Abraham Melchisedec is presented, and he recognizes
him as God's Priest (Gen. xiv.) ere he is justified, (Gen. xv),
and before the main promise of millennial glory is given
(Gen. xxii). But to us the antitype of Melchisedec is
offered ; and it is by the reception of him, that we are
justified and made partakers of the glory to come. Hence
the case of Abraham is introduced at the close of the
parenthesis occasioned by the slowness of the Hebrew
Christians, and the apostle returns once more to the case
of Melchisedec.

The priesthood of Jesus has two phases, the Aaronic
and the Melchisedec ; both of them all-important for
the understanding of the epistle before us. Not to understand the typical bearing of Melchisedec's history on us,
is *dulness of perception worthy of rebuke*. This, therefore,
the apostle administers. For it supposes the loss of the
hope of our calling, as invited to the kingdom. When
Jesus appears as the *kingly* Priest or Melchisedec, our
hope is come.

But Jesus' *present* priesthood is after the Aaronic pattern.
In the Mosaic economy, the high priest was separated from
the king. The Aaronic priest was engaged about sacrifices,
the cleansing of the unclean, the forgiveness of sins. To
reject Jesus as the *Aaronic Priest* then is *utter perdition*.
Such refusers lie under the just wrath of God, for tres-
passes without number. Hence this fearful position
is chiefly depicted, after the Saviour's priesthood, temple,
and sacrifice, as answering to the Aaronic pattern, have
been duly developed. Jesus is seen as the *Melchisedec*
Priest in chap. vii. But his *Aaronic* priesthood forms the
subject of chaps. viii–x. We may be *saved*, though we
are ignorant of, or deny, the Melchisedec priesthood of
Jesus, and his priestly kingdom to come ; as multitudes of

Christians do now. But to refuse him as the Aaronic priest, shuts out from *salvation.*

These two phases of the Lord's priesthood answer to the two rests of the former chapter. To desert Christ as the *sacrificial* priest, is to leave our *present* rest in the righteousness of God. To be ignorant of Christ as the *kingly* priest, is to be ignorant of the *future* rest, or careless about the coming kingdom. The sacrificial priesthood is invisible, exercised in the temple not of this creation, and is received only by the men of faith. The kingly priesthood is to take effect when Jesus appears, when heaven is opened, and both heaven and earth are centred in him.

The history of the Old Testament considered as a typical history of the church and of Christ, is all but closed to us. Any who should attempt to draw aside the veil, however scripturally, would be in danger of being denounced as " fanciful." Even inspired Paul, when he gives us a glimpse of this mode of drawing instruction from the older Scriptures, in the history of Abraham's two wives and sons, has not escaped the unbelieving remarks of some. This temper results from low views of Holy Writ. Christians do not fully believe what they allow, when they confess that Scripture is divinely inspired. They would bind down the meaning of each passage to signify strictly just so much as the writer could discern when he penned it. But this is foolish. The Spirit of God saw far beyond that. *He* dictated the words to convey his own hidden and far-reaching meaning.

Would we then desire that every one should press his views of the typical meaning of Scripture, giving, like Origen, a loose rein to his fancy ? Far, far, be the thought ! God has his meaning in his types, which it becomes to us *discover* in them ; not to impose our ideas upon them. And in order to see our way clearly on this difficult path, we need " senses exercised to discern good and evil,"

It was when philosophy, strong in vain ideas of its own powers, set itself to allegorize, that truths were thrust out from the sight of the professing church, which have scarcely in our day been recovered.

As adults in years of profession, the Hebrew Christians should have sought and relished solid food. They should have had also the vigorous senses of adults, capable of discerning the good and evil tendencies of practices and doctrines. They were quite unaware, how near they had come to an entire defection from the Christian faith. If advancing in knowledge and grace, they would have at once perceived how perilous the position of those who have become careless both of knowledge and of practice. For the two things, as the apostle implies, go together. Where appetite is healthful, there is energy to work, and the senses are alert and vigorous. But when the appetite declines, and the once busy workman sits sluggish and listless disease has begun or will begin, and the end of such disorder may be death.

Chap. vi, 1. " Wherefore leaving the principles of the doctrine of the Christ,* let us go on to perfection ; not laying again the foundation of repentance from dead works, and of faith towards God, of the baptisms of instruction and of laying on of hands† of‡ resurrection of the dead, and of eternal judgment. And this will we do, if God permit."

The connection with the foregoing seems to be—" Since it is disgraceful for adults in age to be living on the food of infants, go onward to the food suited to your age." They ought already to be fully established in those truths which were taught at first to catechumens ; and to leave them as things already sufficiently acquired. That which was taught to those young in the faith was, the first principles of the doctrine of Messiah. What these are, he afterwards proceeds to state.

*Literally, " the word of the beginning of the Christ."
† Βαπτισμων διδαχης, επιθεσεως τε χειρων.
‡I prefer omitting the next τε, with some good MSS.

There are in the Scripture two classes of doctrine; one which lies upon the surface, suited to persons just brought to Christ; and one lying below the letter, or the typical and prophetic one. It is to the deeper doctrine, which he calls " perfection,"* that the apostle invites them onward. Adult doctrine belongs to adults. So Paul assured the Corinthians he had wisdom which he could speak among the " perfect," that is, the adults, or full-grown in the faith: though he was then obliged to administer to them milk only.

What a rebuke is given in the sentiments before us to the Christianity of our day! Not a few, even of ministers, seem to think that there are but two or three doctrines in the Bible. So that the preacher's main duty consists in serving up these in different forms and with various sauces, to deceive the palate! Hence, amongst many on whom Christianity has but a slight hold, there is more or less of disgust. " We want something new! We are ever hearing over and over again the same things." Yet, on the other hand, many are as unwilling to hear new truths as others are unwilling to hear the old. " Teach us what we know," seems to be the silent aspiration and desire of many congregations and churches. Hence the religious publications which have the most extensive circulation, are those which keep to " simple truths." " These things are enough to carry us to heaven; and what would you have more?" A great deal more! This ever-repeated brooding over the first elements of the gospel keeps Christians always children. They understand not the peculiarities of the dispensation in which God has set them, and their conduct, in many respects, shows anything but the peculiarities designed to be manifested by Christianity.

No! this dwelling always on first principles, is not the

---

* Τελειοτης. Paul had, ver. 14, of the former chapter, called those who had advanced in the knowledge of Christ, τελειοι.

doctrine of the Spirit of God. No! "Let us *go on to perfection!*" We are no more to be content with our attainments in the knowledge of Christianity, than in our attainments in grace. Honour, duty, interest, the call of God, must prevent our standing still.

"Not laying again the foundation of repentance from dead works." While, however, the necessity of perfection in doctrine in order to form the "perfect" or adult Christians is enforced, be it far from us to deny the necessity and beauty of first truths. No: they are "*the foundation*"; and, therefore, of primary importance; though the builder is not for ever to be engaged on that part of the edifice.

Paul next specifies the fundamental truths of the gospel.

1 "Repentance from dead works." That was the cry of John the Baptist, the herald of the Christ. "*Repent* ye, for the kingdom of heaven is at hand!" There was indeed in Israel much observance of the law; they kept the external ordinances of Moses with diligence. But their souls were dead to God: and the works that they wrought in their unregenerate state, were "dead works" from which they needed to repent, and to be cleansed, as much as the Gentiles from their idolatries and open profligacy: Heb. ix, 14. But Christians who have attained to the *act* of repentance, should not be for ever needing the preaching of the *doctrine*.

2. "And of faith towards God." This is another aspect of what is demanded of men in turning to God. To the Jew and to the Gentile it was necessary to prove that their deeds were evil, and incapable of saving them. Then came the pouring in of balm into their wounded and troubled conscience: the exhibition of the righteousness of Christ, as that whereby peace might be obtained. This also, in its germ, was taught by John. He directed Israel to "believe on him that should come after him, that is,

on Christ Jesus." Behold, then, the first pair of connected truths.

3, 4. " Of the baptisms of instruction, and of laying on of hands."

Our translators, in the version they have adopted, have wrested the words from their order ; because they could not perceive the meaning of them, as they stood. But the present rendering gives a satisfactory sense. It is also given by the Vulgate. There were two baptisms : the baptism of water, and that of the Holy Ghost. John preached them both, at the very commencement of the gospel. " I indeed *baptize* you *in water** but one mightier than I cometh, the latchet of whose shoes I am not worthy to unloose ; he shal. *baptize* you *in** *the Holy Ghost and in** *fire* " : Luke iii, 16l

And again, " Go ye therefore and *teach* all nations, *baptizing* them in the name of the Father and of the Son, and of the Holy Ghost." Here we have " *the baptism of instruction* " : for teaching was to precede it.

The other baptism is that of the Holy Ghost ; which was ordinarily communicated by the laying on of the hands of apostles. Philip, after preaching at Samaria concerning Christ and his future kingdom, baptized in water those who believed. But, in order that the converts should obtain the baptism of the Holy Ghost, it was necessary for two of the apostles to come down and lay hands on those already baptized : Acts viii. Similarly, we find baptism in the Spirit conferred by Paul upon those already baptized in water. " When they (the twelve disciples of John Baptist at Ephesus) heard this, they were *baptized* in the name of the Lord Jesus. And when Paul had *laid his hands upon them, the Holy Ghost came on them, and they spake with tongues and prophesied* " : Acts xix, 5, 6. The second baptism communicated supernatural gifts.

In some places, the two baptisms are brought into close

* Eν.

juxtaposition. Thus Paul tells the Ephesians that there was, " one Lord, one faith, one baptism [in water] one God and Father of all who is above all, and through all, and in you all. But unto each of us is given the grace according to the measure of the gift of the Christ [baptism of the Spirit]. Wherefore he saith, ' When he ascended up on high, he led captivity captive, and gave *gifts* unto men. (. .) And he gave some *apostles*, and some *prophets*, &c.,": Eph. iv, 5–11. Similarly, Mark xvi, 16–18.

The few who will permit us to speak of the miraculous gifts of old as intended for believers now, call the subject one of " the *deep* things of God." But the apostle thought not so. Far from its being among the doctrines for the perfect in Christ, it is one of the *first principles of the Christian faith !* What marvel that we halt, and are blind without it ?

This is the second pair of closely related doctrines.

5. 6. Of the resurrection of the dead, and of eternal judgment. The resurrection of the dead generally was not taught clearly under the Old Testament. " The ungodly shall not *arise** in the judgment, nor sinners in the congregation of the righteous " : Psa. i, 5. But the New Testament teaches, as one of its first principles, the resurrection of all, whether righteous or unrighteous. " All that are in the graves shall hear his voice and shall come forth, they that have done good unto the resurrection of life, and they that have done evil unto the resurrection of damnation " : John v, 28, 29.

So Paul preaches to Felix, " that there shall be a resurrection of the dead, *both of the just and the unjust* " : Acts xxiv, 15.

The judgment which ensues upon resurrection is to be

* יקמו. Αναστησονται. LXX. Resurgent, Vulg. I connect ' the righteous ' with ' the judgment,' as well as with ' the congregation.' ' They shall not arise at the judgment of the righteous,' as well as have no part in their assembly at the first resurrection.

" eternal." This also is a doctrine first clearly discovered by the gospel. The old Testament threatens nations and individuals with temporal visitation and judgment. But the eternity of the decision when the two great moral classes of mankind arise, was not then set forth. But John the Baptist was at length commissioned to preach it. " He shall burn up the chaff with *unquenchable* fire." The sentence of each, be it observed, takes place, not at death, but at the resurrection.

The words, " And this we will do, if God permit," contain a difficulty. *What* will the apostle do ? And what need of the limitation—" if God permit ? "

There seems a reference to the first exhortation. " Therefore leaving the principles." To which answer those words —" Not laying again the foundation." To the second part of the admonition, " let us go on unto perfection "—corresponds, " And this will we do." The " not laying again the foundation " refers especially to the teacher's part ; as " leaving the principles," supposes chiefly the hearer's. " Let us go on unto perfection," includes both parties ; for, if the hearers are not fit for deeper truths, the teaching is unsuitable. " I will teach you the profounder lessons—do you, on your part, attend." By the apostle's limitation— " if God permit "—I understand him to refer, mentally, to his proposed personal visit, when he hoped to inculcate these more hidden principles : xiii, 19, 23.

4. " For it is impossible for those who were once enlightened and tasted of the heavenly gift, and became partakers of the Holy Spirit* and tasted the good Word of God, and powers of the coming age, if they fall away, to renew them again unto repentance, as they crucify to themselves the Son of God afresh, and put him to open shame."

Let us first speak of the blessings which the passage supposes to be enjoyed by the Christian. They may be divided

*Or of " a holy spirit "—the reference being to supernatural gift.

into two classes—proceeding from the sources previously named : either (1) instruction, or (2) the laying on of hands. The enlightening, and tasting the good word of God, are due to the preaching of the doctrine of Christ. The same word is used of this result : Eph. iii, 9 (*Greek*). The enlightening refers then, as I believe, to the primary instruction concerning repentance and faith, or the danger of the sinner by nature, and his acceptance in Christ. The " tasting the good word of God," has reference to the hopes of the millennial joy. The expression is used when millennial times are described. " behold the days come, saith the Lord, that I will perform *that good thing* (or *word**) which I have promised unto the house of Israel and unto the house of Judah. In those days, and at that time, will I cause the branch of righteousness to grow up unto David, and he shall execute judgment and righteousness in the land " (earth). " In those days shall Judah be saved, and Jerusalem shall dwell safely " : Jer. xxxiii, 14, 15. It is used in a similar sense of the days of Joshua and Solomon, and of the *rest* which God gave to them ; as also of the restoration from Babylon: Josh. xxi, 45 ; xxiii, 14 ; 1 Kings viii, 56 ; Jer. xxix, 10 ; Ps. xxxiv, 8, xlv, 1. It stands opposed, especially in Joshua, to the Lord's threats for breach of his commands, and runs parallel with the blessing and the curse of which Moses speaks.

The three other particulars relate to the miraculous gifts of the Holy Spirit, imparted to the converts, after " the baptism of *instruction*," by means of the " laying on of hands." But why should they be three times described ? Each time a new and important aspect of them as affecting the soul, is brought forward. They are first named, as a " tasting of the heavenly gift."† That word (δωρεα) is always used, so far as I can perceive, of the supernatural bestowments of early Christianity : Acts ii, 38 ; viii, 20 ; x, 45, &c. They probably take this designation first, in

---

* הרבר הטוב.   † Δωρεα.

reference to the first " rest," or to the believer's repose on the righteousness of Christ. The gifts were attached of old to righteousness by faith, as God's seal set thereon : Gal, iii ; Rom. v, 15–17.* There were also appealed to by Peter as the proof of the truth of Christianity, before the unbelieving rulers of Israel : Acts v, 32.

2. It is next called a " becoming partaker of the Holy Spirit." The word employed seems designed, as well as the general meaning of the expression, to lead back our minds to an early quotation in the epistle, where Jesus is said to have been anointed with the oil of gladness above " his *fellows.*"† Now as the head was anointed, so were the members to be. As the Spirit was given to Jesus without measure, so to believers was it granted, " according to the measure of the gift of Messiah." What does " Messiah " or " the Christ " mean ? " The anointed." What does " Christian " mean ? A partaker in the anointing. How inspiring the thought then, of being thus sealed as a member of the Messiah, justified in his righteousness, partaker in his Spirit !

3. But there is yet a third view of them. They were " powers of the coming age." This expression gives the aspect of the supernatural endowments in relation to the millennial glory. And thus it is appropriately connected with that view of apostolic instruction, which disclosed the kingdom to come. Paul couples together the " tasting the good word of God, and the powers of the coming age." They were the pledges and earnests of millennial glory ; they marked out to the eyes of men the heirs presumptive of the promise ; and led Christians, by the prediction of " things to come," to expect the kingdom of Christ as their especial hope.

*I understand by the ' gift of righteousness ' not ' righteousness the gift,' but the gift of the Holy Spirit attached by God to the possession of righteousness.
† Μετοχοι.

Now when any abandoned faith in Christ, after having received these supernatural gifts, he must, in order to make good his case, blaspheme the Spirit whose gifts he had received, as a deceptive and evil Spirit. He must " do despite unto the Spirit of grace," not only by quenching his gifts, but also by that blasphemy of Him, which is declared to be unpardonable.

These things then marked the usual standing of a believer in apostolic days. As the warning is addressed to private believers no less than to ministers of the word, so it describes the position enjoyed alike by each of these classes. That Paul is speaking of believers, is evident. He is endeavouring to preserve true Christians from apostasy to Judaism, not to keep souls newly awakened from falling back to the world. To those merely awakened, and not yet believers, neither the baptism of water nor of the Holy Ghost were administered. Of those just awakened the apostle would not say, that if they fell back to their slumbers, it was impossible that they could be saved. No! there is no escape from the difficulties of the passage, by the theory that persons not really believers are intended. Paul is representing, in awful terms, the peril of finally falling away from inward grace already received.

As there is a partial falling back, involving loss of the millennial kingdom; so a total apostasy, involving eternal perdition, is possible.

But how could he speak thus, consistently with the doctrine of the final perseverance of the saints? It is not necessary to solve this difficulty, ere we believe the obvious meaning of the words. Still I would suggest a thought calculated to diminish, if not remove it. The supposed falling away is not only perfectly POSSIBLE, but *certain*, if the man be left to himself. Yet the truth is, that it has never, and never will be, ACTUALLY REALIZED IN FACT. A thousand things are possible, nay, and really tend to exist, which yet never become facts. It is perfectly *possible*, that

an earthquake might shake down all the houses in the city
of Norwich, leaving only that one standing in which I am
writing ; but no one supposes that it will be. A physician
may say truly to his patient, " Neglect to take the medicine
I have ordered, at the appointed times, and nothing will
save you." Yet he knows full well, that such is the patient's
eager desire to live, that he will not fail to take his pre-
scription. The consequence of neglect then never comes
to pass. The warning given suffices to prevent it.

" If they shall *fall away.*" Not every kind of transgression after faith is here supposed. Nothing less than an
entire and malicious rejection of Christianity for infidelity,
Judaism, or some false religion, is intended. It is quite
parallel with the passage : Heb. x, 26–29. " For if we sin
wilfully after that we have received the knowledge of the
truth, there remaineth no more sacrifice for sins, but a
certain fearful looking for of judgment and fiery indignation
which shall devour the *adversaries.* He that *despised Moses'
law* died without mercy under two or three witnesses. Of
how much sorer punishment, suppose ye, shall he be thought
worthy, who *trod under foot the Son of God*, and *counted the
blood of the covenant wherewith he was sanctified an unholy
thing*, and *insulted* the spirit of grace ? "

The " sinning wilfully " intends the voluntary abandonment of Christianity, as distinguished from giving up the
confession of Christ under terror of death. Here then lay
the mistake of the Novatians, in refusing to receive again
into the church those Christians who had fallen through
fear, or experience of the torture. The case contemplated
by the apostle is an unenforced, persevering, and malicious
abandonment of Christ. It is a *spontaneous* sin, answering
to the " falling away " of the chapter now under investigation. The " enlightening " of the one chapter answers
to having " received the knowledge of the truth," of the
other. It is supposed too, that the apostates in question
are guilty of the blasphemy against the Holy Ghost, which

the Saviour has declared unpardonable. They "insult the Spirit of grace."

They also " crucify to themselves the Son of God afresh and put him to open shame." The first crucifiixon was with God's permission and ordaining. This second cruci-fixion is against his counsel and expressed determination. God hath for ever justified him whom men condemned. For the first crucifiers Jesus pleaded, that they knew not what they were doing. The apostate supposed by the apostle is enlightened, and yet perseveres in his wickedness. He crucifies Christ " to himself "—that is, as far as he can. This is a view of the crime as resting within his own soul. He would slay him again, if he could. He puts him to open shame. This is the aspect of the crime *without*. He leads his enemies to pour forth their blasphemies anew, as if it were quite clear, that Jesus was an impostor, and his religion a crafty fable.

It is to be observed also, that much of the force of the passage turns upon the use of the *present* participle. It is not said, that by an act of sin *presently repented of*, they " crucifi*ed* Christ anew " ; but that they *continue* impeni-tently to crucify him to the close. " They *crucify* the Son of God afresh."

Of such it is said, " it is impossible to renew them again " unto repentance. This must be evident. The impossibility is viewed from the side of the Christian *teacher*. He has no new truths wherewith to affect such souls. The views they have received are exhaustive of the grand motives pre-sented by Christianity. They have known the faith as it discovers present pardon and peace. They have also per-ceived the future glories of the coming kingdom of God. What new motive then shall be brought to bear on such obdurate spirits ? What proofs of the truth of the faith can be given, which they have not already received ? They knew Christ's doctrines. They had the supernatural gifts which " sealed them."

But not only is it impossible for mortal to renew them again to repentance,* but He who alone could, *will not.* Here lies the full impossibility of the case.

Let us now glance at the connexion of this passage with the former verses. " *For* it is impossible." The apostle, in the preceding part, had warned the Hebrew believers of their want of senses exercised to see the tendencies of things. With increasing light and warmth, we become increasingly alive to the danger of conduct whose consequences we once saw not. With decreasing knowledge and love comes insensibility to the peril of final apostasy. To this their danger, therefore, Paul would awaken them—" Go not back in knowledge, for the feeble in knowledge are ever liable to be led astray, and those who are growing cold are tending to that hopeless apostasy which I now depict to you."

7. " For land† which drinketh the rain that cometh oft upon it, and bringeth forth herbage useful for them on whose account it is also cultivated, partaketh of blessing from God. 8. But, if it bear‡ thorns and briers it is rejected, and nigh unto cursing, whose end is to be burned."

The same piece of land, under the same favourable circumstances, is proposed as an illustration of the just wrath of God upon offenders of so aggravated a cast. The soil in question is supposed to be subjected to a twofold beneficial agency; the one, from God; the other, from man. The rain coming oft upon it, is God's. That answers to the believer's tasting of " the *heavenly gift* " of the Holy Spirit. But beside that it is " *also* " tilled by man. That answers to instruction by human teachers.

This supplies the key to the former view of the standing of the Christian. (1) The earthly agency, or the tillage, answers to the " enlightening " of the conscience by the

---

*Observe the parallelism. Μη παλιν καταβαλλομενοι θεμελιον μετανοιας. Παλιν ανακαινιζειν εις μετανοιαν.

† Γη γαρ.

‡ Εκφερουσα δε. The ' if ' is implied in the present case, just as in the former—και παραπεσοντας v. 6.

preaching of God's way of justification. It includes also the farther development of the mind of God by opening "the good word of God" in regard to his kingdom, and glory to those who already believe. (2) The heavenly benefit, or the rain, answers to the other privileges enjoyed by the Christian.

After these agencies of heaven and of earth conspiring to benefit the land, an answerable result of good is expected. The farmer cannot consent to labour in vain. Neither does God permit man to account himself free from responsibility for spiritual privileges and means.

There are then two alternatives as the destiny of the land. The one is favourable. In may reward its cultivators with useful crops of grain or herbs. In that case it is approved of men, and blessed of God. So is it with the Christian, who repays in good works the earthly and heavenly care expended on him. But there is another and evil issue. What, if after all the rain from heaven, and the ploughing, manuring and sowing of earth, it renders back to its occupants thorns only, and briers? What, if for the twofold benefit it returns only a twofold harvest of evil? Then man condemns it. It is rejected. Its cultivation is given up as useless. It is "nigh unto cursing" from God. "*Cursed* is the ground for thy sake"; "*thorns* also and *thistles* shall it bring forth unto thee": Gen. iii, 17, 18.

Its "end is to be burned." The land is set on fire. Its thorns and thistles afford fuel for the flame, and its burning shows man's judgment of its uselessness. Thus, too, it is a type of the doom of the apostate.

What can be done more for land on which every effort of the cultivator has been expended? The exhaustion of every remedy in vain, justly entails destruction as the result.

May we not presume from this, that some of the Hebrew church had occasioned much trouble and grief to their pastors and elders? Is not this hinted in the land that bore to its cultivators only thistles and briers ?   And does not the rejection of such land answer to the exclusion of them from the Church of Christ ?

If now so much is expected from inanimate nature, as the result of means, what may not be demanded from rational and responsible man ?   That believers are intended under both alternatives is confirmed by the description of the land. In each case it has " drank in " the heavenly rain, whether of doctrine or of gift.

This illustration then embraces two extremes ; the case of the apostate, whose end is eternal death, and that of the patient and fruitful believer, who is at length counted worthy of the abundant entrance into the kingdom.   But all consideration of the evil issue ends here.   From this point the true believers or partakers of the first and present rest in Christ are urged on to the attainment of the second.

Thus the two opposites are before us : the movement backward to perdition, or onward to the blessing and glory of God.   It is very observable, that no *example* is given from Scripture of the falling away to perdition ; while, of the second, an example is supplied, and exhortation is founded thereon.

9.   " But we are persuaded concerning you beloved, the better (alternative)* and (that which) adjoins salvation, though we thus speak.   10.   For God is not unrighteous to forget your work, and the love† which ye showed to his name, in that ye ministered, and are ministering to the saints."

In spite of the apostle's fearful picture of the consequences of apostasy, he could comfort them, by assuring them that he believed they were not of that class.   They did not answer, as he trusted, to the evil alternative of the barren soil ; for he knew of the good fruit they had already rendered.   They were the good land, nigh to the blessing ; not the ungrateful ground near to cursing.   He judged by their

* Τα κρειττονα.   † The critical editions omit του κοπου.

good works, as the proof of such tendency. While then good works are not in any degree the ground of our pardon or acceptance, they are the proof of our nearness to enter on the reward of the kingdom, and of a blessed issue to the present life. Do Christian ministers insist enough on the necessity of good works ? " This is a faithful saying, and these things *I wish thee to affirm constantly*, that they which have believed in God might be *careful to maintain good works* " · Tit. iii, 8.

" For God is not *unjust.*" A remarkable expression. It shews that the saints, in regard to recompense, are put under the administration of the Divine equity. Reward will be measured in the kingdom by the rule of justice— " according to works." Jesus receives the chief sovereignty of the kingdom as the supremely *worthy :* Phil. ii ; Rev. v. So in order to our entering the kingdom, we must be " accounted worthy " : 2 Thess. i, 5–11. " The *just judge,*" says Paul, shall give me the crown in the day of Christ. By men, and even by the saints who receive them, our good works may be forgotten, as Mordecai's good deed was by Ahasuerus, and Joseph's by the chief butler. But it is not so with God. Far be it from him that he should remember our provocations, and not also those works of obedience, which bring glory to his name !

As the bad land yielded a twofold crop of evil, they, as the good land, had yielded, and still did yield, a twofold crop of good. They returned love to God, and service to the saints, as the requital of the earthly and heavenly culture.

Observe the nature of the good works commended. They were not simple acts of philanthropy, but works of love to the *saints*, springing from the love of God. These give evidence of our being heirs and children of the kingdom. To one of these good works—the spreading a feast for the poor who cannot repay—a remembrance and reward in the kingdom is definitely promised : Luke xiv, 14. Nor shall the simple cup of cold water, given to a disciple because he belongs to Christ, fail of its reward : Matt. x, 42.

The terror of the picture drawn by the apostle had its use, in keeping the saints from conduct which would certainly, if pursued, end in their destruction. Nevertheless, he consoles them by the cheering hope, that that awful fate would not be theirs. If a child were obliged to be left in the presence of arsenic, it would be well to say to it—" Eat that arsenic and you will die." While yet, if the child were frightened at being left in the room with it, we might add— ' Be not afraid, you will not eat it, and it will not hurt you.'

11. " But* we desire, that each of you should manifest the same diligence to the end, with a view to the full assurance of hope. 12. That ye become† not slothful, but imitators of those, who through faith and patience inherit the promises."

But if Paul were so hopeful of them, wherefore his rebuke ? Because, while the labour of love was still performed by many, some were slothful. They neither sought to do works acceptable to God, nor to grow in knowledge. Each, he hoped, would show the same diligence as the most zealous among them. Their diligence also was to be *constant*, " diligence to the end." And the exhortation is enforced on each individual. It is *singly* that we shall give account to Christ. " *Each* shall bear his own burthen."

This diligence had two ends in view, an immediate and a more distant one. Diligence was to be exhibited, as a means to the attainment of a fully assured hope of the glory of God. The more self-denying, patient, and diligent we are in the service of our Lord, the stronger is the confidence with which we regard ourselves as the children of God ; and the better reason have we to look for the joyful entrance into the kingdom : 2 Pet. i. It is, then, the doctrine of the passage before us, that confidence of millennial glory is to be attained by perseverance in a holy and beneficent life. Assurance grows brighter with increasing obedience.

* Δε.   † Γενησθε.

The assurance spoken of is not the assurance of *faith*, but the assurance of *hope*. Faith rests on the general assertions of God. These are made to certain characters. But that *we* have fulfilled those descriptions of the inheritors of reward is a matter of *hope*: which hope may, and does, grow brighter in proportion to obedience.

The distinction between the two kinds of assurance may be seen by comparing this passage with the other which speaks of Abraham's assurance of *faith*. " Being not weak in faith, he considered not his own body now dead, when he was about an hundred years old, neither yet the deadness of Sarah's womb ; he staggered not at the promise of God through unbelief, but was strong in faith giving glory to God, and being fully *assured*,* that what he had promised, he was able also to perform " : Rom. iv, 19–21. Here the promise respected solely *God's power*, and Abraham's belief was the full assurance of *faith*. But that we shall be accounted worthy of the coming kingdom, is a matter of *hope*.

They are moreover admonished, that they should not become slothful. Again they are gently reminded, that they did once run well. So strong was their confidence once, that they bore with perfect calmness, nay with joy, their being stripped of earthly goods. They were well assured that they had a better property on high. As then it was disgraceful to fall back, they are urged to return to their former works. How necessary is this appeal to Christians still ! We ever need to be warned, not to become " weary in well doing." The temptations around tend to cool Christian zeal. And some believers seem even to value themselves thereupon, and pity those youthful Christians, who are running in the ardour of their first love, as inexperienced younglings, who by degrees will sink to their temperature of frigidity and experience. But Christ

---

* Πληροφορηθεις.

rebukes such cold-hearted ones : and assures us, that the lukewarm are nigh to being spued out of his mouth.

They were to be " imitators of the inheritors of the promises." This introduces the example of Abraham, and prepares for a return to the history of Melchisedec. Abraham, and those resembling him, are inheritors of the promises. That is, they have the full and recognized title to them. God has enrolled their names for the coming glory : though they are not yet in possession of it.

This possession of an interest in the promises made to Abraham was to be regarded, not as a matter of sovereignty, but as a thing to be sought and attained, " *through faith and patience.*" The apostle proceeds to show, that thus Abraham attained his part in them ; and as he is the father and model of God's dealings towards believers, it is an exhibition how we are to make sure our interest therein.

13. " For when God made promise to Abraham, since he could not swear by any greater, he sware by himself, saying,

14. 'Surely blessing I will bless thee, and multiplying I will multiply thee.' 15. And so, after having patiently waited, he obtained the promise."

The connexion with the former part seems to be as follows—" When I desire you to seek to inherit the promises, I assure you, that they are indeed an inheritance. For they rest upon oath, and that the oath of God. The oath, too, of which I speak, was given as the reward of Abraham's perseverance in faith and good works." The apostle desired, that they, by diligence on their part, should attain to the assurance of hope. But there may be full confidence in things of the world, which, as it rests on unstable and untrusty persons, is disappointed. The Holy Ghost, therefore, designs to prove the certainty of the possession, as far as God is concerned.

The occasion to which the apostle refers, is worthy of all consideration. God made this oath to Abraham (Gen. xxii, 17) after his offering up his son Isaac. It was the last covenant which Jehovah made with Abraham.

In chap. xv, Abraham is declared to be justified on the simple ground of faith. The Most High promised him a single heir, and a seed numerous as the stars. Abraham believed, against the promptings of the flesh, and of unbelief. It is Abraham's *passive* obedience herein, which is the basis of the apostle's argument in Romans iv. God next demanded of his servant *active* obedience to the command of circumcision. That was immediately rendered. He was tried, afterwards, by the promise of a son of Sarah. In that he believed passively, and it was fulfilled. But the last and sorest trial of his faith, was the demand that he should offer Isaac, the son of the promise, upon a distant mountain. On his submission to this, the oath of God was granted. " Faith and patience " had had their perfect work. Hereupon the Most High testifies his approval of his obedience by his angel. " Now I know that thou fearest God, seeing thou hast not withheld thy son, thine only son from me." But the angel utters his voice the second time. " By myself have I *sworn* saith the Lord, *for because thou hast done this thing and hast not withheld thy son, thine only son*, that in blessing I will bless thee, and in multiplying I will multiply thy seed, as the stars of heaven, and as the sand which is upon the sea shore ; and thy seed shall possess the gate of his enemies : and in thy seed shall all the nations of the earth be blessed ; BECAUSE THOU HAST OBEYED MY VOICE." Here, therefore, the unchangeable covenant of God stands attached to Abraham's *obedience*.

Abraham was justified by *faith only ;* but after justification, God looked for the *fruits of obedience.* His servant's faith is tried for fifty years : and at the close of that period, the Holy One affixes his oath of promise to his last act of obedience. This, then, is exactly in the strain of the previous exhortations of the apostle. " Be imitators, ye sons of Abraham by faith, of his noble example. You have begun your career, like Abraham your father, justified by faith. But from you, as from him, God looks for obedience, ere he pledges himself by oath to you, as he did to him, that you shall be of the inheritors of the kingdom of his seed, which is Christ. It you persevere, like Abraham, up to the last surrender he requires, you shall have, both in your own soul, and on God's part the full assurance of being included in that oath wh:ch opens the door of millennial blessing."

For the covenant by oath refers to the day of the kingdom of Christ. As the former oath of *exclusion* was levelled against the *disobedient;* this of *admission* introduces the *obedient.* The words of the covenant of Gen. xxii, evidently will be fulfilled in the millennial day. 1. The day of Abraham's own full blessing will be when he rises from the dead, and "sits down" with "Isaac and Jacob in the kingdom of God." For that he looked. Then will God fully approve himself as the *God* of Abraham, according to Jesus' words to the Sadducees. Then will Abraham's double seed be seen : his seed like the stars, in the bright glory of those in heaven, clothed unchangeably in their bodies of resurrection : and his seed like the sea sand, the earthly posterity in possession of Canaan. Then will his seed possess the gate of their enemies. We, Abraham's spiritual seed, shall then be victors over the spirits and principalities of darkness on high, against whom now we wrestle. They will then for ever be cast down from on high. Then, too, the Gentiles smitten before Israel, will become their servants ; and Esau, or Edom, the especial enemy of Israel, will be "for a possession." Then, in Christ, the individual "seed" of the promise, all nations will be blessed : and grace will flow down, through the two-fold seed of Abraham's faith and Abraham's flesh, to the inhabitants of earth.

Now as the oath of exclusion applies to us, so much more does the oath of promise and admission on obedience.

While the example of rejected Israel stands as a beacon to warn us against loss, so does the example of Abraham stand to encourage us.

But the apostle draws our attention to the form of the oath. God sware " by himself." The reason was, that he had none greater to sware by. An oath is the calling in of some superior, as witness and avenger, in case of the breach of the conditions. But God could call on no superior. Behold, then, the immutable guarantee of the promises to Abraham ! Even a man's covenant may not be altered, but by agreement of both parties ; much less an oath. How unchangeable a basis of security then is the oath of God !

The oath covenants *blessing* to Abraham. " Bless- ing I will bless thee." Abraham, then, was the good land, that yielded useful herbs : and the issue was, blessing from God. We find also two stations from which blessing flows to Abraham : an earthly and a heavenly. (1) Abraham is blessed on *earth* by Melchisedec—" And he *blessed* him, and said, *Blessed* be Abraham of the Most High God, possessor of heaven and earth." (2) Also the *heaven* opens, and the angel from on high promises blessing. When Abraham is blessed on earth, he is vic- torious over his foes of earth : but when he is blessed from heaven, he has the type of *resurrection*, in the rising up of his son Isaac from off the altar : Heb. xi, 19.

The oath embraces Abraham *and his seed ;* and Abraham and his seed *as children of obedience.* Isaac was no less obedient to the heavenly mandate than his father. Herein then was given a type of Abraham and his obedient seed blessed in resurrection. Both are included in the oath. " Blessing I will bless *thee.*" " Thy *seed* shall possess the gate of his enemies."

" And so after he had patiently endured, he obtained the promise." But how is that ? Does not this epistle, a little further on, assert of Abraham and others, that they "all died in faith, *not having received the promises*" : xi, 13, 39. Yes, but the reconciliation is not difficult. Two different words are used in the two cases.* Here the apostle means, that Abraham received the *bare word* of the promise. He denies his having yet received *the thing signified*, or the accomplishment of the promise, in the later passages.

He had indeed patiently to endure in faith. From the time of God's first calling him up to the time of the oath, was a space of fifty years! His case then is just the reverse of Israel's. Abraham and Abraham's sons after the flesh were both tempted or tried by God. Abraham was called to leave Ur, as his children were called to leave Egypt. Both obeyed : but that was not the end of their trial. Abraham was tempted in the chapter just noticed. And at Sinai Moses savs, "God is come to prove (or tempt†) you" : Ex. xxi, 20; Deut. viii, 2. But "by faith Abraham when he was *tempted*, offered up Isaac" : Heb. xi, 17. Isaac when proved in the desert, by unbelief tempted God. An opposite issue attended conduct so opposite. *Abraham inherited the promise under oath, Israel under oath is shut out of the promise.* Even thus the believer's conversion is not the end, but only the beginning of his trial by God. If he tempt God and provoke him in place of obeying, he is nigh to being shut out of the kingdom.

Here then are our two examples. We must either, after coming to Christ, be living as obedient Abraham, or as disobedient Israel. After reaching a certain extent of obedience or of provocation, we fall under either one or the other of the two oaths of God. God must ever be true to himself. His word is living still, and applies to us as truly as to Israel or to Abraham. Faith sets us on the course : but patient perseverance in well doing is the way to the goal.

---

* Επετυχεν here, προσδεξαμενοι and κομιζεσθαι in the other place.
†Same word that is used of Abraham, Gen. xxii, 1.

16. "For men indeed sware by the greater, and the oath is unto them an'end of all contradiction, with a view to confirmation. 17. Wherein God wishing more abundantly to manifest to the heirs of the promise the immutability of his purpose, interposed by an oath. 18. In order that by two immutable facts* wherein it was impossible for God to lie, we might have strong consolation who have fled for refuge, to lay hold on the hope set before us."

The apostle refers to the customs of men. The oath, whether of declaration or of promise, is the last guarantee that can be given. A man is pledged by his word. Many, however, scruple not to break it. But if dependence can be placed on any, it is when he has called on God to witness to his words, and to avenge the breach of them, if he should break them. So when Jacob obtains the sale of Esau's birthright, he is not content with Esau's promise, he adds, "Swear to me this day, and he sware unto him": Gen. xxv, 33.

But does not this passage prove the lawfulness of oaths to a Christian? Many have thought so; but surely, it does not. The Holy Spirit here is simply stating the *customs of men in general*, a custom which was acknowledged and sanctified by God's commands under the Law.

But the command of the Law of Moses stands repealed by Jesus to Christians. "*I say unto you, swear not at all.*" And much less can the customs of *men* be a law for *believers*. On the contrary, it is the condemnation of Christians to "walk as *men*": 1 Cor. iii, 3.

But may we not swear, if God himself does? No: not if he forbids it. Besides, God's oaths were all of them sworn in previous dispensations; there is no instance of an oath sworn by the Most High since the coming of his Son.

Since then men lean for security on an oath, as the very strongest tie whereby they can bind their fellows, God, in his mercy, condescended to stay the feeble, fluctuating faith of his people, by that security. The promise then becomes

* Πραγματων.

absolute ; dependent on no condition of man's fulfilling. And Almighty power stands up to accomplish the promise of eternal truth. Well then might Abraham fall asleep in peace on such a pillow as that ! The Lord of life shall raise the dead ! His changeless counsel shall one day have its conspicuous performance. Could Bathsheba repose with confidence on David's oath to her son Solomon, and plead it in full assurance before him, though another was then claiming to reign ? Could Jacob die with comfort when Joseph had sworn to carry " up his bones out of Egypt ? " How much greater may be our confidence, that the last and greatest enemy of Messiah shall be overthrown ! and that the Lord will make us victorious by his own victory in resurrection !

The argument next turns upon the promise then made under oath to Abraham and his seed. The seed are " the heirs of the promise." This oath and promise, it is assumed, are like the former oath, as yet in force, and applying to *us*. Are we then " the heirs of the promise ? " Yes, as far as our standing in Christ goes. But the apostle has proved, both here, and in the previous case, that our obedience is required, in order to our entering into the promise. The promise to Abraham now in question, is the limited one of millennial glory. *Eternal life* is infinitely beyond the desert of the obedience of any mere man. The attainment of *that* is solely of gift. But it has pleased God to appoint a thousand years as the time of recompense for our deeds. " The promise " to Abraham in Gen. xxii, refers to the same period, as " the rest " held out to our hopes in chapters iii and iv. " The immutability of his counsel," relates to his determination to bring in the kingdom of his Son triumphant over the kingdoms of the earth. From age to age, and from dispensation to dispensation, this one great counsel of God has been kept in view. It has taken different forms, according to the wisdom of God, but the purpose has remained unchanged throughout.

In order to comfort the saints, God "*interposed* by an oath."* An oath is a sort of mediator between parties at variance, to end doubts and strifes. God then set his oath as a sort of mediator between himself and his purpose, that all doubt or dispute as to the certainty of the performance of it might be at an end.†

To this oath given to Abraham those inspired by the Holy Ghost turn, as soon as the gospel begins to appear in the horizon "To perform the mercy promised to our fathers, and to remember his holy covenant, *the oath which he sware to our father Abraham*, that he would grant unto us, that we being delivered out of the hand of our enemies might serve him without fear, in holiness and righteousness before him all the days of our life" : Luke i, 72–75. But these words view the promise to Abraham only as it applies to the Jews, or the earthly people.

God then has sustained his promise by two immoveable "facts." And what are they ? (1) The promise or covenant ; and (2) the oath. The promise of blessing and multiplying Abraham and his seed had been given long before Gen. xxii, under the form of a covenant or promise : Gen. xii, 2 ; xiii, 16 ; xv, 5. That was one fact. The oath is the other. And these two " facts " or covenants are of different kinds. The covenant by word was conditional, and received by faith. The second or oath, was unconditional, and had respect to Abraham's inheritance and to God's good pleasure in his works and patience.‡ But Abraham's life, as the father of the faithful, is a pattern for

---

* Εμεσιτευσεν ορκῳ.

†The oath to Christ, that he should be a priest of Melchisedec's order, will be fulfilled in its entire extent, in the same millennial day. Then Christ will be the *kingly* priest.

‡When God covenants on his word, the sacrifice of animals is made the pledge : (Gen. xv.) When he covenants on oath, there is the type of a better sacrifice, in the offering of Isaac ; and also the type of resurrection, on which the better covenant is founded.

us also, as exhibiting the ordered dealings of God with the children of faith.

Now God cannot break his word, much less his oath. But the Holy One desired his people to have the most secure foundation for their hopes, under the troubles to which their faith called them. And this is needed amid the difficulties and seeming impossibilities of its performance, especially since the performance of it has tarried so long.

For God calls his people not only to faith, but to patient waiting for the promise. But what are difficulties to him, on whose will all power attends? The raising of the dead is as nothing to him. Herein lies our hope. Here is the fulfilment of the promise.

But who are "the heirs of the promise?" "We, who have fled for refuge to lay hold on the hope set before us." Those only are heirs of the promise who, as having Abraham's faith have given up all hope of righteousness in themselves; and perceiving themselves deserving of the wrath of God, have left the vain shelter of their own deeds. In the word "fled for refuge," there would seem to be an allusion to several of the histories of Scripture.

1. Noah's ark was a refuge, and the family of Noah fled into it with the hope of escaping the flood, and with the promise of God's covenant as their hope.

2. Again, in the history of Abraham, there is an account of a fleeing for refuge. The mountain was pointed out to Lot, as the place to which he was to direct his flight, when long-deserved vengeance at length lighted on Sodom.

3. But the cities of refuge seem to me to be more in the eye of the apostle. To one of these the manslayer, who had unintentionally killed any one, was directed to flee. His life was insecure in every place but that.

The avenger of blood might pursue and kill him without sin, anywhere but there. This has ever been regarded as a beautiful type of the gospel. But there is one circumstance which binds the figure very closely to the main subject of which the apostle is treating. Before the manslayer, when once he had entered into the city of refuge, was set a *hope* of returning back in peace to his home. It was made dependent on the death of the *high priest :* Num. xxxv, 25 ; Josh. xx, 6. And it is with the *priesthood* of Jesus, as offering *present refuge* and *future hope,* that the Holy Ghost is now engaged.

Christ, as the priest after Aaron's type, is now in the temple above ; having offered the sacrifice of atonement, on which our present acceptance and rest before God, depend. Here then is *present refuge* in Christ's present priesthood. For though Christ be a priest after *Melchisedec's order,* yet his priesthood, as at present exercised, is after the *Aaronic pattern,* as the epistle goes on to show. For Melchisedec, as far as we know, had no temple ; nor did he offer sacrifice. But it is on the priesthood of the Saviour, " after the order of Melchisedec "—the kingly and priestly offices combined on earth—that our *hope for the future* depends. The present rest in God is due to the present priesthood of the Lord : our future rest, to the future type of his functions.

4. Perhaps also there is a reference to that refuge at the horns of the altar, to which some malefactors betook themselves. Thus, in Solomon's day, Adonijah and Joab fled to the temple, and laid hold on the horns of the altar. To Adonijah it served as a refuge ; and Solomon gave him a hope of life : 1 Kings i. But Joab, though he took refuge there, was there slain as the murderer. Perhaps in this we have an image of the doom of the wilful apostate.

19. " Which (hope) we have as an anchor of the soul both sure and steadfast, and entering into that within the vail. 20. Whither Jesus as the forerunner entered for us, having become a high priest for ever after the order of Melchisedec."

The hope set before us is the first resurrection, or " the glory of God " in his kingdom. This hope, as above the world, and springing from a source not affected by its changes, steadies the soul. As the anchor often prevents shipwreck, so does this hope retained, keep us from being overwhelmed by the storms of life. It enters within the vail, for thither has the risen Jesus entered. To Abraham was given the oath of God on the Mount of earth, but the reality of resurrection has been fulfilled in Christ, in the holiest of the heavenly places. Our hope then is far more advanced towards completion, than when Abraham's faith rested on God's word in his day. We have now a sure pledge of the fulfilment. The High Priest of Aaron's line entered only into the holy places made with hands, and only in the strength of natural life. But Jesus has entered into the heaven itself " for us." He is our forerunner, gone before to prepare a place. We are both on the same road ; but he has arrived first, to get ready mansions in the Father's house for us.

Come then what may, the oath of God must be fulfilled and his kingdom appear ! The anchor of the ships of earth may break, or its cable give way, or the fluke lose its hold. But our anchor is " sure," and will not break ; it is " steadfast," and will not lose its hold of the rock to which it is grappled. Other anchors are cast downward, and lay hold on the regions below. But ours is on high, fixed in the heavens, fastened to the very throne of God.

The high priest of old entered into the holiest to make atonement, but not to abide there himself, much less to make preparation for the entrance of others to the presence of God.

What lessons then does this portion of Scripture inculcate?

1. Cultivate deeper knowledge of Scripture and of Christ. There may indeed be knowledge without correspondent practice : but there will not be right practice without correspondent knowledge.

2. Be careful to maintain good works. They are the signs of being a child of the kingdom. They are a token of your being nigh to the blessing promised to the good land.

Believer, would you have the full assurance that the promises of millennial glory are yours ? Be diligent ! As with advancing knowledge and increasing grace are conjoined confident expectation of the blessing, and the assurance of hope ; so, with declining grace come ignorance, indifference even to the first principles of the gospel, and the peril of final apostasy. The Lord give his people more of Abraham's faith and patience ; yea, grant them to tread in the footsteps of Jesus ! While works do not save us, they are yet ever telling on our account, ever looking forward to the day of recompense. May we seek to be rich in them !

CHAPTER V

THE TWO MOUNTS

HEB. xii, 12–29

THE latter half of the twelfth chapter of the Hebrews is one of the most difficult passages of the New Testament. Though I would be far from affirming that its full meaning is known to me, yet some points in it are clear enough. It bears evident testimony to the great truth—that the actions of the saint have a direct bearing upon his future reward and destiny. Let us with reverent hearts consider its teaching.

12. " Wherefore lift up the hands which hang down, and the feeble knees. And make straight paths for your feet, lest that which is lame be turned out of the way, but let it rather be healed."

The Holy Spirit thus takes up the figure of a race with which the chapter began. " Wherefore let us too,* seeing we are compassed about with so great a cloud of witnesses, lay aside every weight, and the sin which doth so easily beset us, and *let us run with patience the race that is set before us*, looking into Jesus the author and finisher of our faith." The intermediate verses are occupied with considering the intention of God in sending afflictions on his people. Such afflictions had long fallen on the Chris-

* See Greek.

tians among the Hebrews, and they had had the effect of depressing their spirits, and of well-nigh causing many of them, in their despair, to turn back to Judaism.

They were like fatigued runners, whose hands, once in rapid motion by their sides, now hang down listlessly, and whose knees tremble, from long-sustained exertion. They were like Israel journeying around Mount Edom " The soul of the people was much discouraged because of the way " : Numb. xxi, 4. And perhaps they were not far from breaking forth into those murmurs which the tribes then uttered, and which drew down from the Lord the plague of the serpents.

Like a wise shepherd therefore Paul encourages the flock. He takes up the sentiment, and nearly the words, of Isa. xxxv, 2–4. " They shall *see the glory of the Lord, and the excellency of our God. Strengthen ye the weak hands, and confirm the feeble knees.* Say to them that are of a fearful heart, Be strong, fear not, behold *your God will come* with vengeance, even *God with a recompense ; he will come and save you.*" The subject of his consolation is the coming of God to reward his people, and to destroy their enemies. Such had been the object which the writer had set before his readers in chaps. ix and x of this epistle. " *To them that look for him he shall appear the second time,* without sin unto salvation " : ix, 28. " For yet a little while, and *he that shall come will come, and will not tarry.* Now the just shall live by faith, but if he*draw back, my soul shall have no pleasure in him : x, 37, 38.

In the passage too that is now engaging our attention, our " seeing the Lord " is made the object of hope, and the motive to renewed exertion, for he will reward his faithful ones at his appearing, as he himself also has been rewarded : Heb. xii, 2 ; Phil. ii.

" And make straight paths for your feet." This is apparently a quotation from Prov. iv, 26, as given by the

*The insertion of the words " any man," is unjustifiable.

Septuagint. It requires of those within the church, and especially of the rulers of it, a straightforward policy, and a consistent life. The paths of the wicked are crooked paths, and they know not at what they stumble : Isa. lix, 8 ; Prov. ii, 15. There were, among the believing Hebrews, some who were " lame." They were halting between Christianity and a return to Judaism. A very little might turn them away from the faith. The misconduct of those within the church would be a powerful motive, in the hand of Satan, to draw them aside to their ruin. The leaders of the church therefore were to remove all stumbling-blocks out of their path ; to be guilty of no crooked acts of policy, lest the weak should say—" If this be the faith in Christ, the old scheme is better. I have done with the new " To the tendencies to apostasy from without, were not to be added motives from within the church. Rather to the rulers of the church the word of Isaiah applied. " Cast ye up, cast ye up, *prepare the way, take up the stumbling block out of the way of my people* " : Isa. lvii, 14.

Towards the weak in the faith, the ministers of the gospel were to use patience and exhortation, seeking to heal and to restore. The strong are apt to be impatient towards those ready to stumble, and the dull of understanding ; and too ready to say of the sickly of the flock —" He gives more trouble than he is worthy of—let him go ! " But such is not the spirit of Christ. " *Let him rather be healed !* " If a believer, he is deeply valuable in the eyes of the Lord. Love will care for the feeblest of the fold.

14. " Pursue peace with all, and holiness, without which none shall see the Lord."

The first exhortation was to hold fast the faith ; this, to retain the life becoming a believer. The figure too of a runner is still retained. " Pursue after peace." The command to seek peace, seems a carrying out of the former exhortation; the demand of holiness which succeeds, links on the previous exhortations to what follows. Love and unity are the especially needful graces of the church of Christ. Where these abound, the church prospers. Where quarrels are rife, the holy are disquieted and despairing; the lame are turned aside. Therefore this follows at once on the preceding injunction. Nothing is more repulsive to those halting between Christianity and the world, than the strifes of believers.

We are therefore to "pursue after peace." It is not always attainable. But it is always to be sought after. Peace too "with *all*," with the world, as well as with the church. All but the truth may be given up, in order to "maintain the unity of the spirit in the bond of peace."

The present command is found also in Psa. xxxiv, 14. It stands connected with the promise of good days; that is, of the kingdom of Christ. With this view, it is cited by Peter: 1 Pet. iii, 10, 11.

"And holiness." This is to be ever the object of the Christian's pursuit. He is not to be satisfied with the measure whereto he has attained. Holiness is always attainable, for we seek it of him who is willing to give. But peace is not always capable of being maintained; for we have at times to do with those, who, when we speak of peace, make ready for war.

The necessity of holiness as the preparation for the presence of God was prefigured in the history of Israel. "Lo," said God, "I come unto thee." Go unto the people, and *sanctify* them to-day and to-morrow, and *let them wash their clothes*, and be ready against the third day; for the third day the Lord will come down in the sight of all the people upon Mount Sinai": Ex. xix 10, 11.* That was typical of the inward holiness de-

*Is there, in the exhortation to peace, and to take care of the weak, any allusion to Amalek's attack on the feeble and stragglers ere the reached Sinai ?

manded now of the people of God. We stand in the same position with them, expecting the descent of the Lord Jesus from on high. A higher sanctification then becomes us, for we are not merely to see his descent at a distance, but to be caught up into his presence. And answerably thereto, there were two visions of God at Sinai: that of the people in general, and that of the seventy elders, who entered into the presence of the Lord beyond the cloud, and feasted before him.

The pure and the peace-makers are amongst those to whom an entrance into the kingdom will be granted, as the beatitudes (Matt. v.) teach us.

15. "Taking the oversight* (of one another) lest any come short of the favour of God†, lest any root of bitterness springing up trouble you, and thereby many be defiled. 16. Lest any be a fornicator or profane person, as Esau, who for a single meal sold his birthright."

From the first words of the verse before us, it appears, that believers are not only to regard their own individual salvation, but also to watch over the good of others. Each member of the body is to esteem the welfare of all an object of his desire, and of his pursuit, according to the measure of ability granted to him.

For various perils beset the Christian, three of which are noticed here. The first is —

"Falling short of the favour of God."† The meaning of the expression may be one of the two following:

1. It may mean a falling back from the external or exhibited grace of God under the *Gospel*, to the justice of God as exhibited in the *Law*. The gospel is the dispensation of the manifested grace of God. Peter testifies that "this is the true *grace of God* in which ye stand": 1 Pet. v, 12. It was Satan's desire, and the aim of their fellow-countrymen, the unbelieving Jews, to bring them under the yoke of Law again. Against that Paul warns

---

* Επισκοπουντες.　　† Υστερων απο της χαριτος του Θεου.

the Galatians. Christ had become of no avail to whoever sought to be justified by law, they had " *fallen from grace.*"* So Paul exhorts the disciples just gathered at Antioch in Pisidia, to " continue *in the grace of God* " · Acts xiii, 43. It is in this sense that at the close of the chapter it is said, " Let us hold fast grace."

2. But it may mean, " losing the favour of God " : the contrary to that frequent expression in the Old Testament, of " finding favour " with any. And then to " lose the favour of God," will mean to fall under his displeasure. This latter is, I believe, the true sense of the expression.

We have several phrases in this epistle and elsewhere, which answer to such a view. Thus in a passage before quoted, " The just shall live by faith, but if he draw back, *my soul shall have no pleasure in him* " ·

" Wherefore," says the apostle to the Corinthians, " we are ambitious.† that whether present or absent we may be *well-pleasing to him* " : 2 Cor. v, 9.. And again, at the end of this epistle, he prays that God would work in them " that which is *well-pleasing* in his sight " : Heb. xiii, 21.

On the plea of finding favour with God, Moses rests his request to *see the glory of God :* Ex. xxxiii, 12, 13, 16, 17, 18. That example evidently lies close to the point before us. The Holy Spirit has just before made known what is necessary to our seeing the Lord.

The phrase imports then a previous state of favour before God, and the danger of losing that favour by misconduct. The case is somewhat parallel, in regard to the expression and the position of the two parties, with that given in Deut. xxiv, 1. " When a man hath taken a wife and married her, and it come to pass, that she *find no favour in his eyes,* because he hath found some unclean-

---

* Τῆς χαριτος εξεπεσατε.
† Φιλοτιμουμεθα.

ness in her " Probably also there is reference to Ex.
xxxiii. "And Moses said unto the Lord—See, thou
sayest unto me, bring up this people : and thou hast
not let me know whom thou wilt send with me. Yet
thou hast said, I know thee by name, and thou hast *found
grace in my sight.*" Thereon he founds his plea for favour
to be shown to Israel. " Wherein shall it be known that
I and *thy people have found grace in thy sight?* Is it not
in that thou goest with us ? " Israel had then lost their
position of favour before God, by idolatry. Moses, as
the Mediator, sought to restore it.

With the feeling also as it exists in the mind of God
is connected the manifestation of that feeling in the day
of recompense. Thus we have elsewhere the similar
expressions : " All have sinned, and *come short of the glory
of God*" : Rom. iii, 23 " Let us therefore fear, lest a
promise being left us of entering into *his rest,* any of you
should seem to *come short of it* "* : Heb. iv, 1.

That saints, whose sins of the past are forgiven, may
so far lose God's favour, as to fall under his temporary
displeasure, in seen by the example of Aaron and Miriam.
Because of their speaking against Moses, Jehovah called
them before him, and rebuked them. " Were ye not afraid
to speak against my servant Moses ? " " *And the anger
of the Lord was kindled against them :* and he departed,"
leaving Miriam leprous : Numb. xii, 8–10. Yet Aaron
was " the *saint* of the Lord " · Ps. cvi, 16. And Miriam
is mentioned with honour, as one sent before Israel : Mic.
vi, 4.

If we take the expression in question in the first sense,
it would suppose the falling into apostasy, and the lying
under the curse. But in the second sense a variety of

---

*The same verb is used in both these cases as in the passage
under notice, υστερεω. In the use of this word there
seems a reference to the previous faintness of heart already
noticed. They are as stragglers outside that camp in which the
favour of God dwells.

degrees of fatherly displeasure may be supposed; all
compatible with final salvation.

We have now arrived at the second caution expressed
by the apostle. "Lest any root of bitterness springing
up trouble you, and thereby many be defiled." The first
warning is general; the two following point out special
sins. There are two classes of sins, answering to two
well-known families of diseases. There are some which
attack individuals only: there are others which are con-
tagious or infectious. and spread, as from a centre, around
a still increasing circumference. The last kind is the
one against which the Hebrew Christians are first warned
to exercise watchfulness. There was danger of the rising
of infectious sins amidst the believers of Palestine. By
"the root of bitterness" may be meant either (1) the rise
of false doctrine spreading from one to another; or (2)
the formation of parties ranged against one another, and
engaged in unseemly and destructive strifes.

The heart of the believer is compared to land which
bears beneath its surface many seeds and roots of an
evil and noxious nature. They only need the encouragement of neglect on the part of the rulers of the church,
and the fostering influences of opportunity, to show themselves above ground in leaf and fruit. Such sin while
concealed, is a *root* of bitterness. But, if cherished, it
sends forth *words;* as the root throws up its buds. If
not checked, it proceeds to evil *deeds*, which are the fruit.
Of that fruit many may eat, to their loss and sorrow.
Such cases need oversight. Taken at once, the mischief
may be stayed, but if suffered to grow, it takes deep root,
and perhaps at length defies a remedy. The biters and
devourers of one another are at length consumed of one
another.

To those who resist, the spreading evil is a source of
trouble: but to the many who are caught by it, it is a
source of *defilement.* As then even the worldly proverb

says, that "Prevention is better than cure," the wisdom of God thought fit to rouse the church and its officers to watchfulness.

The history of Israel in the wilderness again lends us light in illustration of the warning before us. (1) Of this character was that rebellion against God, which resulted in the idolatry before the mount. The thought of unbelief, that Moses would never return, arose in not a few minds. One spoke out the thought to his neighbour, and he to a third, till all were ready to demand an object of sight that might be their visible leader. How many were defiled by this root of bitterness! (2) Of like character was the rebellion at Kadesh Barnea. The secret fear of going up into the promised land after being fanned by the unbelieving words of some, invaded the whole people, and all the spies but two, till the congregation grew fierce, and would have stoned the faithful ones. (3) Such was the rebellion of Korah, Dathan, and Abiram, against the authority of Moses and Aaron. Probably the whole of that sin found its centre and source in Korah. His pride prompts him to whisper to a few whom he thought like-minded with himself, some word of bitterness against the leaders appointed of God. The spirit spreads: each newly infected one increases the disorder, till the whole congregation are gathered together against God and his servants: and evil thoughts, words, and deeds defile the whole camp. How great the displeasure of Jehovah at these roots of bitterness, is apparent enough from the summary blows of indignation which he dealt upon those defiled thereby.

It may further be observed that the words now under notice are a silent quotation from Deut. xxix. That and the succeeding chapter exhibit a *new covenant*, beside that made in Horeb. It rehearses God's previous mercies to Israel, as seen in his treatment of Pharaoh and Egypt, and his kindness to them as the people of God, during the

H

march through the wilderness. On the ground of favour shown to them, they were to keep the present covenant. If they kept it, they were to be the people of God. God had sworn to Abraham to make them his people. But they were to prove themselves sons of Abraham by obedience, else they would come under God's oath to cut them off from the rest. For the Lord feared—

1. "*Lest there should be among you* man, or woman, or family, or tribe, *whose heart turneth away this day from the Lord our God,* to go and serve the gods of these nations." How like the caution expressed in the early part of the present epistle !—" Take heed, brethren, *lest there be in any of you an evil heart of unbelief in departing from the living God* " : iii, 12.

2. " *Lest there should be among you a root that beareth gall and wormwood,* and it come to pass, when he heareth the words of this curse, that he bless himself in his heart, saying, I shall have peace, though I walk in the imagination of my own heart, to add drunkenness to thirst. The Lord will not spare him, but then the anger of the Lord and his jealousy shall smoke against that man, and all the curses that are written in this book shall be upon him, and the Lord shall blot out his name from under heaven " · 18–20.*

The deceit of the heart in promising itself that all would be right at last, in spite of deliberate acts of transgression, was a disorder that infected some of the people of God of ancient days, and might corrupt some of his people under the gospel. Against it therefore a protest is entered, and a solemn warning. The wrath of God would fall heavily on such turning of the grace of God into licentiousness.

16. "Lest any be a fornicator, or profane person as Esau, who for a single meal sold his birthright. 17. For ye know that afterwards, even when desirous of inheriting the blessing, he was rejected ; for he found no place of repentance, though he sought it earnestly with tears."

*Does Jesus refer to this passage in Rev. iii, 5 ?

That saints may be guilty of fornication is but too clear ; both by mournful facts, and by Scripture "I shall bewail many which have sinned already, and have not repented of the uncleanness and fornication, and lasciviousness which they have committed " · 2 Cor. xii, 21. What then shall be the result of such sins, committed after faith, and the profession of the name of Christ ? Shall it not hereafter affect the standing of the guilty party ? Is there no punishment beyond that of spiritual coldness and deadness *now ?* Scripture gives a very different testimony. It assures us that such, though they may finally be saved, will have no part in the Saviour's kingdom of the thousand years. " Be not deceived, neither *fornicators,* nor idolaters, nor adulterers, nor effeminate, nor abusers of themselves with mankind, nor thieves nor covetous, nor drunkards, nor revilers, nor extortioners *shall inherit the kingdom of God " :* 1 Cor. vi, 9, 10. "For this ye know, that no whoremonger nor unclean person, nor covetous man, who is an idolater, hath *any inheritance in the kingdom of* (him who is) *Christ and God " :* Eph. v, 5. The kingdom mentioned being that of the Christ or Messiah, shows it to be the temporary kingdom which Jesus will take as the Son of David, the Messiah of the Jews.

It appears as if even positive punishment would be adjudged to saints guilty of this sin. "For this is the will of God, even your sanctification, that ye should abstain from fornication, that every one of you should know how to possess his vessel in sanctification and honour ; not in the lust of concupiscence, even as the Gentiles which know not God. That none go beyond or defraud his brother in the matter (*marg.*) BECAUSE THAT THE LORD IS THE AVENGER OF ALL SUCH, *as we also have forewarned you and testified.* For God hath not called us unto uncleanness, but unto holiness. He therefore that despiseth, despiseth not man, but God " : 1 Thess. iv,

3–8. " Whoremongers and adulterers God will judge ":
Heb. xiii, 4.

God's anger against this sin was seen in his treatment
of it under the law, as is pointed out to us in Paul's summary of the Lord's ways with his people of old : 1 Cor. x.
Moses likewise notices this point, when he is recalling
to his people the Lord's dealings with them : " Your
eyes have seen what the Lord did because of Baal-peor,
for all the men that followed Baal-peor, *the Lord thy God
hath destroyed them from among you* " : Deut. iv, 3. The
service of Baal-peor was connected immediately with
Israel's unholy intercourse with the daughters of Moab :
Numb. xxv.

" Or profane person, as Esau." It is not intimated,
I believe, in spite of the close linking of the present with
the former sin, that Esau was guilty of fornication. But
the sins are classed together, because they are both a
virtual bartering of the great glory prepared of God, for a
paltry present return.

Esau is characterized as " profane " and fully does his
history bear out the charge. He " sold his birthright."
What was contained in the " birthright " is not in every
point clear. Under the law, a double portion of the father's
estate belonged to the first-born : Deut. xxi, 17. And
when the father was a king, the kingdom descended to
him naturally, unless the Lord, as supreme governor,
was pleased to ordain otherwise : 2 Chron. xxi, 3. But
in Esau's case, we may see what he lost, by observing what
afterwards became Jacob's The Most High inserted
the name of Jacob into his own title. Jehovah was " the
God of Abraham, Isaac, *and Jacob.*" He is often called
" the God *of Jacob,*" or " the God of *Israel* " alone. That
glory then was rent from Esau the profane. From Jacob
too sprang the twelve patriarchs, and Messiah himself.
On the basis of those twelve tribes is founded the kingdom
of God ; and their names are lastingly engraven on the

gates of the eternal city of God. To give up spiritual advantages then for earthly ones is the part of profaneness ; and of that crime Esau was guilty in the sale of his birthright.

But he was further guilty in the trifling remuneration of a worldly kind which he accepted in exchange. It was a "single meal." It had been profaneness, had he claimed to be supported by Jacob all his life long, as the price of the surrender. But to part with it for the gratification of an hour, was the extreme of profaneness. He himself speaks slightingly of it when he sells it. "Behold, I am at the point to die, *and what profit shall this birthright do me?*" Men in general cry up the value of the goods they are about to sell ; but Esau himself depreciates the pre-eminence he was about to dispose of. He sells it, too, with an *oath*, calling on God to bear witness to the wicked transaction. Behold another shameful aggravation of the sin ! To the account of the sale the Holy Spirit adds, "He did eat and drink, and rose up, and went his way." He went about his usual employments when the meal was over, as though he had done nothing of any particular importance. He showed no sign of penitence, either then or afterwards, till the time of bestowing the blessing. "*Thus Esau despised his birthright.*"

Observe, however, the extent of the sin. It was not by Esau's falling into idolatry, and wholly renouncing the God of his father, that the loss of the birthright took place. Nor was it by disowning Isaac as his father. Isaac still recognises him as his son, though he is compelled to withhold the blessing of the first-born. The example of Esau then is a lesson to the *believer*, to one who will be acknowledged by God in the day of recompense as still his son.

The issue of the case is made a warning to us. Esau at length desired the blessing. When his father was about to bestow it, he endeavoured to obtain it. But it was withheld from him by the providence of God.*

The Lord held Esau to his bargain. He was a witness called in to the sale, and by his providence he prevented Isaac from bestowing the blessing on Esau. When he found that his brother had procured the blessing for himself, " he cried with a great and exceeding bitter cry, and said unto his father, " Bless me, even me also, O my father ! " But Isaac was not won over to repent of his words, or to recall the blessing. " I have blessed him, *yea and he shall be blessed !* " " And Esau lifted up his voice and wept." Though therefore he at length sought the blessing even with tears,† he obtained it not. He could not get his father to repent of the pre-eminent honour given already to his younger brother. " *He was rejected !* "‡

But how does the example apply to ourselves ?

1. First, Esau was a descendant of Abraham, and the circumcised son of Isaac. Herein he corresponds to believers now. He was as truly a son as Jacob. To all appearance, his was the birthright. It would have been duly bestowed at length, but for his misconduct. We then are in a like position. As born again of God, we are presumptive heirs of the kingdom. As believers in Jesus before the millennial day, and ere the bringing in of Israel, we are the first-born. This then is not a lesson to unbelievers.

2. Profane conduct, like Esau's, will cause us to forfeit entrance into the kingdom, which is the birthright pro-

---

*We have no need to defend the conduct of Jacob either in buying the birthright, or in seeking to obtain it by fraud. It was evil in God's sight, and as such punished. But that is not the point before us.

†" He sought *it.*" This may grammatically refer, either to (1) the blessing, or to (2) the change of his father's purpose. But I prefer to understand it of the latter.

‡ Απεδοκιμασθη. This is an instance then of one becoming αδοκιμος—" a castaway "—a thing which Paul feared for himself : 1 Cor. ix, 27.

posed to us. We may barter the future and spiritual blessing for the present and earthly. In thousands of cases has this profane sale taken place, and it is to this day transacting in every varied form.

(1) Here is a believing minister, who sees that such and such doctrines and practices of his denomination are unscriptural. Sorely they wound his conscience. But what is he to do, if he gives up his present station, and the living which he derives from it? What profit shall his birthright do him, if he is to surrender his present sphere and maintenance? Thus argues his unbelief. And under the influence of that unworthy motive, he continues in a position which he feels to be sinful. How does such a proceeding differ from Esau's? In principle, not at all. The worldly benefits then which such a one receives by the maintenance of his faithless position, are the mess of pottage. They are the price which he obtains by the sale of his birthright. God will keep him hereafter to his bargain.

(2) Here again is a Christian tradesman. He finds that some of the practices of his trade are unchristian and evil. But how can he act differently from his ungodly neighbours? If he wishes to "*make a fortune*," as they do, he must act as they, or he will be left behind in the race. He perseveres therefore in such doings, till his conscience grows callous. What shall we say then? Is not this Esau's profane bargain over again? Whether such perceive the reality of the barter or not, God will hold them to the exchange made. They have received their good things now. They have obtained them by the sacrifice of spiritual interests. When therefore the time of reward comes, their virtual sale will be remembered. It was a real, though not a formal bargain. It proceeds upon *low thoughts of the promised glory of God.* It is like Esau's contempt of the birthright, manifested by his actions.

3. To such, the day of recompense will present anew the scene between Esau and his father. Esau, in spite of his sale and oath, *fully expected to receive the blessing of the first-born.* When finally rejected, he speaks like one robbed of his due. But the Lord took care that he should be rejected. Thus will all those Christians be treated who, like Esau, stand by their profane exchange of things spiritual for things temporal. They will, at length, when the kingdom and glory of Christ are come, awake to the perception of the value of the blessing, and to earnest desires after it. But the bargain must stand. The kingdom cannot be theirs.

One more firm than Isaac will keep to his word. They will find no repentance in him. They have enjoyed their mess of pottage—they shall not have that, and the birthright too. The inheritance was sold by them. They have stood to the bargain all their life, and now God holds them to its consequences.

Observe the most forcible point of the representation : IT IS A TRANSACTION BETWEEN A FATHER AND A SON. Yes, the *Father* refuses the blessing to a *son.* He refuses it to his *favourite son.* Despite natural and special tenderness, Esau's cries and tears are vain. Take heed then, Christian, though a son of God, that you do not, by undervaluing your birthright, at length sell it. If you do, One, unchangeable in justice and holiness, will exclude you as profane, from the thousand years of Messiah's glory. For, mark well, Esau did not retire from his father's presence with a *curse*, he simply lost the blessing which he bartered away. It fully answers therefore to the recompense to a saint.*

Chapter vi. offers to us the result of a holy and obedient

---

*This example of Esau stands connected also with the warning " Lift up the hands that hang down, and the feeble knees." It was under the influence of weariness, and the despair of unbelief, that Esau parted with his jewel.

life in the case of Abraham. Esau gives us the opposite result. It is the pattern of God's dealings at the coming of Christ, with those of his children who have offended against him by acts forbidden.

18. " For ye are not come unto the mount that might be felt and to kindled fire, and gloom, and darkness, and tempest, and the sound of trumpet, and the voice of words, which (voice) they who heard intreated that not a word more should be added to them. For they endured not the prohibition,—' And if a beast touch the mountain it shall be stoned.'*—And, (so terrible was the spectacle,) that Moses said, ' I am terrified and trembling.' "

How the example of Israel, exhibited in these words, stands related to the foregoing text, is far from obvious. Yet, that it is intimately connected, the word " for," with which the paragraph begins, bears witness.

The case of profaneness has been specially settled, and illustrated by the example of Esau—the issue of his conduct being set before us in a sentence commencing with the same conjunction.

I am apt to suppose, that the present casual particle stands related to ver. 14. ' Follow holiness, without which *none shall see the Lord. For* ye are not come to the mount of terror, but to that of faith and grace. You are drawn to obedience by the cords of love applied to sons, not driven to it by the lash of justice applied to disobedient slaves.'

The Lord is about to appear, as he promised also to Israel at Sinai. But he demands holiness of you, as truly and in a higher sense than he did of Israel. He is both just and gracious. These two attributes form essential parts of his character. He will display both of these in his future intercourse with his people. The " for " in both cases introduces the notice of recompence to come.

The scene above described is taken from the history

---

*The words which follow do not rest on good authority, and are omitted by critical editions.

of Israel at Sinai. But it is more intimately allied to Moses' view of it given in Deuteronomy iv, v, than to the simple historical account given in Exod. xix, xx.

Seven phenomena are noticed as combining to create the terrors of Mount Sinai. They are partly sights, partly sounds.

1. The mount is denominated, "the mount that might be touched." One is apt at first to imagine that we should read, "the mount that might *not* be touched." But the point designed to be noticed by us is, its sensible nature. It was offered not only to sight, but placed within the range of that most circumscribed of our senses—the touch. Many things we can see which we cannot touch. Who can reach the horizon, or the stars ? But that mount was close at hand, unlike the mount proposed to faith. The command not to touch it involved the power to do so.

2. "And kindled fire." This seems especially to have terrified Israel. It was a sign of God's indignation. It is said, eight times over, that God spoke to them out of the midst of the fire ": Deut. iv, 12, 15, 33, 36 ; v, 4, 22, 24, 26. "Ye were afraid, says Moses, *by reason of the fire*: v, 5. Twice it is said that "the mountain burned with fire " ; "for the Lord descended upon it in fire " ; God showed them "his great fire."

3, 4, 5. "Blackness, and darkness, and tempest." Thus the LXX give the three Hebrew words, which are rendered by our translators, in Deut. iv, 11, "darkness, clouds, and thick darkness."*

6, 7. "The sound of trumpet, and the voice of words." These were the *sounds* of terror, as the others were the *sights* that caused alarm. The voice was God's. This is more than once pressed on Israel's attention. "Did ever people hear the *voice of God* speaking out of the midst of the fire as thou hast heard and live ? " Deut. iv, 33.

One element of that terrible scene is omitted in the

---

*Σκοτος, γνοφος, θυελλα. Deut. iv, 11, and v. 22.

present specification, but it is only to be taken up afterwards, for it has a future aspect.

Such was the alarm created by this sublime spectacle, that the hearers excused themselves from hearing the words of God any more. They were afraid, lest the great fire which they beheld, should consume them.

The commands too which Moses brought before the Lord descended were calculated to inspire great dread. The mount was to be fenced off, that none might touch it. And if even a beast touched it,* it was at once to be put to death. Whence the inference was inevitable —if even an ignorant and irrational beast be thus smitten, what shall become of the human wilful transgressor?

Nay, and even Moses, the mediator of the Old Covenant himself, whom they asked to go up to God, and to hear his words, was terrified, and expressed his fears. It is asked—Where this is asserted, in the account of the descent of the Lord on Sinai? It must be answered,— Nowhere: though it seems not improbable that the occasion may have been that noticed in Exod. xix, 19. "And when the voice of the trumpet sounded long and waxed louder and louder, *Moses spake*, and God answered him by a voice." Then might Moses have expressed his dread, and have been encouraged by the Lord.

But, if not, how should the Holy Spirit be at a loss in teaching us what occurred on that day? A *human* writer could only know what Moses has written. But He who was to bring all things which Jesus had said to the remembrance of the apostles, could find no difficulty in telling us what Moses felt and said.

22. "But ye are come to Mount Zion, and to the city of the living God, the heavenly Jerusalem. 23. And to myriads of

---

*As the Greek word that answers to—" If a beast *touch* the mountain "—is quite different from that used in " the mount that might be *touched*," I have expressed the difference by two different English words. Different *senses* belong to them.

angels ; to the festival and church of the firstborn that are enrolled in the heavens ; and to the Judge, the God of all, and
to the spirits of just men made perfect. 24. And to Jesus the
Mediator of the new covenant, and to the blood of sprinkling
that speaketh better things than that of Abel."

In the above verses a contrast is drawn between the
things presented to the Jews at Sinai, and those now
set before us. Under the old covenant a mountain,
evident to the senses, was set before Israel, whereon fire
flamed and law came forth, moving all hearts to terror.
From it the people were fenced off by the threat of death.
This covenant when developed in its fulness, took as its
centre Jerusalem the earthly, whose inhabitants were in
bondage to the law and its curse, having earthly promises
as its hope.

But, under the new covenant, an unseen Zion in
heaven, and a heavenly city are offered to the eye of faith.
From it proceeds grace, leading believers to the love of
God, and promising perpetual life in resurrection. From
that mount and city we shall not be fenced off ; but shall
enter in and dwell there in God's peculiar presence.

We are waiting at the foot of the mount for the descent
of our Lord and God. He has gone up like Moses, and
we know not when he will return. The blood of the covenant has been shed, and we are in expectation of being called
up, like the elders, to appear before God. But let us consider the objects that characterise our mount more minutely.

They are eight in number ; the number of perfection
in resurrection, as seven was that of the law. They consist
of sights and sounds, as under the law. But they are
pleasing to faith. Our hopes are as superior to those of
the old covenant as our priest, temple, and sacrifice are.

1. We have come to *Mount Zion*. This is a real
mountain, though as yet unseen. It is an object to faith
alone. But John was set upon it, when he beheld the
heavenly Jerusalem : Rev, xxi, 10. The earthly Jerusalem
and its Mount Zion are types of the heavenly city and its

mount. It is seen again, Rev. xiv, 1. The mountain to whose foot Israel was brought was tangible ; ours cannot be touched, nor be an object of our sight, save in resurrection.

2. "And to the city of the living God, the heavenly Jerusalem." The title of "*the living God*," is designed especially to bring before us God's power in resurrection. When Peter confessed Jesus as "the Son *of the living God*," Jesus spoke of his own resurrection, and of his recalling the church from the gates of Hades ; that is, from the power of death by resurrection. Jerusalem the earthly is, in one sense, the city of God, but it is not the city of God as the giver and maintainer of eternal life. The true city of God will for ever exclude death : Rev. xxi, 4.

For this city, we are told, Abraham looked. It was to be his in resurrection. It was a city "whose builder and maker is God." But it is a real city ; not an airy shadow, designed to figure some unknown, celestial blessedness. No : it is the "abiding city," "the city to come," for which the men of faith are seeking : Heb. xiii, 4. And as the men of faith under the old covenant looked for it, and we look for it also, so at length it is the common centre in which we meet : as this paragraph shows.

In Gal. iv, Paul speaks of Abraham's two wives as representing two covenants ; and their sons as the subjects of those covenants. Hagar the bondwoman, had Sinai as her mount ; and as her city, Jerusalem the earthly ; whose sons were then in bondage to the law.

But Sarah answers to the new covenant ; whose mount is Zion, whose city is the Jerusalem that is to come ; and whose citizens are freemen. "Jerusalem which is above is free, *which is the mother of us all*." The two scenes then which the apostle presents before us in Hebrews are another exhibition of the two covenants and their respective standing. The old covenant had no city on the top of its mount. It was nothing but a barren crag. But with our heavenly mount is conjoined the heavenly city.

3. "And to myriads of angels." Angels were present on Mount Sinai, at the giving of the law. "The chariots of God are twenty thousands, even thousands of angels: the Lord is among them, as in Sinai, the holy place": Psa. lxviii, 17. But there they were present as legislators: in the city to come, they appear as companions and fellow-servants of the saints.

4. "To the festival* and church of the firstborn enrolled in the heavens." It was the glory of Jerusalem that the tribes were required to go up thither to keep God's feasts there before him. In this respect, too, our Jerusalem and its feasts will be superior. Angels and the ransomed of mankind will both meet there. Israel kept at Sinai the passover in the second year: Numb. ix, 1-5. There too were the firstborn assembled, who were spared by the paschal lamb's blood, when the firstborn of Egypt were smitten. But the firstborn of the new covenant take a higher standing than those of the law. The passover is to be fulfilled in *the kingdom of God:* Luke xxii, 16. The heavenly festival then will be the real one, of which the earthly was but the shadow. Those of Israel were numbered by Moses, and probably registered by him: Numb. iii, 40, 42. But these are "enrolled *in heaven.*"

But who are meant by "the assembly of the firstborn enrolled in Heaven?" I suppose that the church is intended. We are "the first trusters in Christ": Eph. i, 12. We are "a kind of first-fruits of his creatures" James i, 18. Jesus is declared "the firstborn," at the commencement of the epistle: Heb. i, 6. And we are to be associated with him as his "fellows": v, 9. The firstborn were the

---

* Πανηγυρις. In the LXX it is thrice given as the translation of מועד or feast: Ez. xlvi, 11; Hos. ii. 11; ix, 5, and once of a cognate word: Hos. v, 21.

most nearly connected with the blood of the lamb, and in a peculiar sense redeemed by it. Israel was God's firstborn on earth ; the church takes that place on high. Thus, too, the case of Esau is seen fully to apply to us. To us, as the firstborn, belong " the rights of the first-born,"* unless by our sin we lose it.

5. " And to the Judge, the God of all."† This trans-lation gives the order in which the Greek words stand. But there is a difficulty in understanding their force. (1) God as the Judge may be regarded as the distributor of the prizes to the successful candidates in the race. With this figure the chapter begins. In this sense Paul speaks of Christ as " the righteous *Judge*," who shall award him the crown : 2 Tim. iv, 8 ; 1 Cor. ix, 24, 25. (2) Or it may represent the judge as " the God of *all* " in allusion to the scene at Sinai. God assumed at Sinai his title as derived from Israel. Though all the earth and its nations are his, he would yet regard Israel as his peculiar people, and be called *their God*. But now he is the God of all ; and will in the age to come appear to be so. Hence angels, the church, and just men made perfect, are here found conjoined. God is the God of them all. And judgment is taken in this sense in our epistle : Heb. x, 27–30 ; ix, 27 ; xiii, 4.

6. " And to the spirits of just men made perfect." By the just are meant, I suppose, the saved of the law. " A just man " was the appropriate title of one who pleased God under the law ; Prov. iv, 18 ; Luke ii, 25 ; xxiii, 50 ; Matt. xxiii, 29 ; 2 Pet. ii, 8. So in the account of the worthies of the Old Testament in the preceding chapter, it is said of Abel that God testified of him that he was " just " : Heb. xi, 4. The cloud of witnesses spoken of in the eleventh chapter were " just by faith," and ob-tained testimony because of it, but received not the thing promised ; " God having provided some better thing for

* Πρωτοτοκος. Πρωτοτοκια.   † Και κριτη Θεφ παντων.

us, that they without us should not be *made perfect* ":
xi, 40. They are waiting for us. And we are waiting for
" the adoption, to wit, the redemption of our body." It
would appear then that they are contemplated by faith as
already united to their bodies. Then God will appear in
the full sense as " the God of Abraham," when he rises
from the dead. For Abraham's spirit is not the complete man. Abraham is the compound being, made up
of body and soul. This is the force of the Saviour's answer
to the Sadducees.

7. " And to Jesus, the mediator of the new covenant."
The fifth and following chapters have been engaged with
Jesus as the Priest of the new covenant. But now we
are come back again to the Saviour, as the antitype of
Moses. Moses was afraid to draw nigh. Jesus has sat
down in the heavenly place itself. Moses was unable to
make atonement for the sin of Israel, Jesus has effected a
reconciliation for the sins of the former covenant, as well
as for those of the present and future dispensations.

8. " And the blood of sprinkling, which speaketh better
things than that of Abel." The allusion is to the blood
of the sacrifices which Moses offered at Mount Sinai,
when the old covenant was made. " And Moses took
half the blood, and put it in basons : and half of the blood
he sprinkled on the altar. And he took the book of the
covenant and read in the audience of the people : and
they said, all that the Lord hath said will we do, and be
obedient. And Moses *took the blood and sprinkled it on
the people*, and said, behold the blood of the covenant which
the Lord hath made with you concerning these words "
Ex. xxiv, 6–8. The blood of Christ is spiritually sprinkled
on the hearts of believers. " Let us draw near with a
true heart in full assurance of faith, having our *hearts
sprinkled from an evil conscience*," for we have " boldness to
enter into the holiest by the blood of Jesus " : Heb. x, 22.
So 1 Pet. i, 2.

There was no sin in the shedding of the sacrificial blood, wherewith the old covenant was ratified. But in shedding the blood on which the new covenant is founded, greater guilt than that of Cain was incurred.

But though Abel's blood cried out for vengeance against his murderer, the blood of the new covenant brings peace and forgiveness, even to those guilty of the death of the Son of God. This blood embraces the people of God in their twofold character, as those of the old covenant and of the new. The city, the Judge, the Mediator, and the blood are common to both : Heb. ix, 15.

The example of Esau showed the necessity of holiness to our future welfare. But the example of Israel now before us, discovers to us the results of holiness as a matter of duty imposed by a superior. It is especially designed to exhibit the sad consequences, to those who turn away from grace to the justice of God as meted out by law.

In order to discover most clearly the connection, a tabular view will be most advantageous.

A	B
	Watching—
1 Lift up the faint hands.	1. Lest any fail of grace.
2. Make straight paths.	2. Lest any bitter root spring up.
3. Follow { peace holiness that you may see the Lord.	3. Lest any be { a fornicator profane like Esau. For you know the issue to him.

I suppose then that as the first " for " takes up the three or four cases in the table B, so the second " for " has special reference to the three or four cases presented in table A.

Accordingly the passage commencing with the second " for " begins with encouragement. " Lift up the faint hands, *for* you have not come to Sinai and its wrath, but to the heavenly Jerusalem." Also, the implied threat, "without which none shall see the Lord," answers as precisely to the case of Israel, as rejection from the birthright, to the case of Esau.

25. " See that ye refuse not the speaker. For if they escaped not, who refused him that spoke divine oracles* on the earth, much more (shall not we escape) if we turn away from him (that speaks divine oracles) from the heavens. 26. Whose voice shook then the earth ; but now he hath promised, saying, ' Yet once more, I shake not only the earth, but also the heaven.' 27. Now that (word) ' Yet once more,' manifests† the removal of those shaken (heavens and earth) as having been (already) created ; that those not shaken may remain."

Under the old covenant there was " the voice *of words*." Under the new covenant there is " the voice *of blood*." But of Abel's blood it was said, " *The voice of* thy brother's *blood* crieth to me from the ground. And now art thou cursed from the ground." But the voice of this blood, is pardon and blessing to the guilty. How significant the difference ! Yet Israel, the antitype of Cain, is now a wanderer with God's mark set upon them, through the nations !

' Listen then ever,' says the apostle, ' to the voice of that blood ; ever you must need it. Ever must you abide under its shelter, till the angel's sword is past. Be not weary of its voice, as Israel was of God's speaking at Sinai. In some degree .they were excusable then : so loud and terrible was the voice, so stern and severe its demands. But such excuses cannot now be made for any who reject the word of the Gospel. It is the voice of mercy.'

Yet, with all the apparent modesty of Israel's request, there seems to have lurked beneath it enmity at the holiness of God. While then it proved that the design of God to produce fear in their hearts had been fully answered, and so far was acceptable to him ; yet it was the fear of the slave and of the rebel. To this secret import of their words God seems to allude, even when he

---

* Χρηματιζοντα. † Δηλοι.

confesses them to be right: Deut. v, 28, 29. " O," says he, " that there were *such an heart in them* that they would fear me, and keep all my commandments always, that it might be well with them and their children for ever." Does not that sentiment imply the Lord's knowledge, that thev would not act up to their promises, through the treachery of their heart ?

" For if they escaped not, who refused him that spoke divine oracles on earth." From the time of the ratification of the covenant on Mount Sinai, all offenders were smitten. Their refusal of him who spoke from the earthly Mount of Sinai was not direct and positive ; it was an excusing of themselves ; an objection, not to the thing demanded, but only to the mode of its exhibition. Yet that petition availed not to deliver them from the penalties of their deeds. Much less will those escape who refuse the light yoke of Christ. The aggravation of the guilt of such is noticed from two points of view. (1) The superior place now taken by the utterer of the holy oracles. Israel heard God, after he had descended on the Mount : we hear him from heaven. (2) They excused themselves, from the mode in which the heavenly oracles were offered to them. They sought for a Mediator ; for one in human form and with human voice, who should deliver to them the commands of God. But the parties here warned were in danger of " *turning away*," not only from the words of the speaker, but from the speaker himself. Now " turning away " is the act of entire rebellion and of apostasy. The Lord had forbidden the faithless Israelities to go up into the land, after his word was passed. But they would go up to battle, in spite of Moses' warning. " Ye shall fall by the sword ; because ye *are turned away from the Lord*, therefore the Lord will not be with you " · Numb. xiv, 43. " But if thine *heart turn away*, so that thou wilt not hear, but shalt be drawn away, and worship other gods, and serve them " : Deut. xxx, 17. See also Deut. xiii, 5. Prov. xxviii, 9.

Hence, when the better covenant of grace is made with Israel, it is promised that Israel shall not turn away from God as truly as he will not turn from them "And I will make an everlasting covenant with them, that *I will not turn away* from them to do them good ; but I will put my fear into their hearts, *that they shall not depart from me*" : Jer. xxxii, 40. Also iii, 19.

The turning away from Christ is far worse than Israel's, then. They turned from the awful voice of God to a human mediator. But all who desert the Gospel turn from a mediator at once human and divine, and from his blood who has made peace. Now to such, says the Spirit, there remains no more sacrifice for sins, but only an expectation of fiery vengeance : Heb. x, 23–31. Was Israel smitten, though they turned from the thunders of justice ? Much more those who despise the dispensation of mercy. And if even the *spectacle of* justice was so terrible, what shall be the *endurance* of the wrath of God for ever ? If the unwitting touch of the mount by a beast was to draw down instant death, how much more the wilful rebellion of the human transgressor ?

The Speaker *then*, and the Speaker *now*, are the same person. The speakers are only contrasted (1) with regard to their places, and (2) the consequences of their voice. Jesus is the speaker now. He speaks in two ways. (1) By his blood from earth. (2) By his voice from on high.

A different style of cleansing was required then from that demanded now, owing to the different standing taken by the Great Speaker. Before, when speaking on earth, he demanded an earthly cleansing of the exterior. But that cleansing soon passed away. Now, as speaking from heaven, he requires a heavenly and an abiding cleanness ; even purity of heart.

But the speaker being the same both then and now, holiness is still demanded of the people of God, under all dispensations. " Sanctify yourselves, for the Lord is coming to visit you," was the message of God to Israel. Such also is the message to us of the present dispensation. The nature of the Lord remaining the same, his love of holiness must abide. He requires to be obeyed as truly now as then. " If ye will hear his voice, harden not your hearts." The motives to holiness and obedience then were fear, and earthly promises ; the motives to the same conduct now are love, and heavenly promises. The rejectors of the words of God under each dispensation will meet his just wrath. The grace which is preached now, does not give licence to the transgressor ; does not argue, that hereafter there will be no penalty on the wilful apostate ; nay, the very reverse. The apostle concludes on the contrary, that *severer* justice will seize upon the wilful deserter of the gospel.

As compared with the example of Esau, we may observe, that the former illustration seems to refer to the immoralities or grievous offences of one who does not give up Christ and the gospel ; while this latter example is intended to terrify those meditating total apostasy.

Had the example of Israel been stated in the same mode as that of Esau, it would have taken some such form as this :—" Take heed that you refuse not the voice of God, as did Israel at Sinai ; for you know, that in spite of such refusal, they were subjected to punishment." But the differences of the circumstances needed to be stated ; and this has altered the form into which the apostle has thrown the warning.*

But we are next directed to consider the effects of the speaker's voice on the things around. Its effects on *men*

---

* The analysis of the example is as follows :—

1. The terrible appearances on Sinai. 2. The voice of God. 3. Israel's excusing themselves.

In the new covenant we have :—

1. The joyful appearances. 2. The voice of blood. 3. The warning not to excuse ourselves.

have been considered. But, beside that, the voice of God at Sinai shook the earth. "The whole mount," says Moses, "*quaked greatly*": Exod. xix, 18. Herein then we have a refutation of the ordinary comment on these words. It is asserted, that the shaking of heaven and earth means "the unhinging of the civil and ecclesiastical polity of the Jews, and the abolishing of the Mosaic dispensation." But was the earth that was shaken at the giving of the covenant of Sinai a polity? Was it not the literal earth? And if it was so, the heavens and earth yet to be shaken are the literal heavens and earth.

But the speaker has now removed to heaven. As his voice when on earth shook earth, so his voice from heaven shall shake heaven and earth. That voice has not yet been heard; but it is "promised." It will not be the gentle voice of command, as given in Scripture. It will be the shout of his descent in fire, on the day of his coming. It will be far more awful than that on Sinai. Yet it is spoken of not as a threat, but a foretelling of good. The quotation is taken from Haggai. Haggai discovers to us Israel's delay in building the temple; and God's command that it should be rebuilt. Though the temple in his day was poor in comparison of its splendour in the day of Solomon, yet the latter glory of the house should be greater than the former."* Yet once, it is a little while, and *I will shake the heavens and the earth*, and the sea, and the dry land; and I will shake all nations, and *the desire of all nations shall come, and I will fill this house with glory*, saith the Lord of Hosts." "The glory of this house shall be greater, the latter than the former, saith the Lord of Hosts, and in this place will I give peace, saith the Lord of Hosts": Hag. ii, 6, 7, 9. The shaking

---

*. We should not read "latter house," but connect "latter" with "glory." "The glory of *this* house shall be greater, the latter than the former, saith the Lord of hosts"; ii, 9; see also v. 3.

of all nations, and of heaven and of earth, is *preparatory to the coming of Jesus, and his filling the temple of Jerusalem with glory.* It must take place at some time after this dispensation. For God will *there,* as the Lord of the armies of heaven, give *peace.* But at his first coming, and during the present dispensation the Saviour refuses to grant it. "*Think not* that I am come to send *peace on earth;* I came *not to send peace, but a sword*" : Matt. x, 34.

But there is in Haggai a second prophecy of the shaking of heaven and earth. The latter of the two is especially in the eye of the apostle, in his concluding exhortation. "Speak to Zerubbabel, governor of Judah, saying *I will shake the heavens and the earth,* and I will overthrow the throne of *kingdoms,* and I will destroy the *strength of the kingdoms of the Gentiles,* and I will overthrow the chariots, and those that ride in them ; and the horses and their riders shall come down, every one by the sword of his brother. In that day, saith the Lord of Hosts, will I take thee, O Zerubbabel, my servant, the son of Shealtiel, saith the Lord, and will make thee as a signet ; for I have chosen thee, saith the Lord of Hosts : " 21–23. In these words we have the destruction of the power of the Gentiles, and the restoring of power to the chosen governor of Judah. Thus the shaking of heaven and earth is not only a promise to the saint, but to Israel. It occurs, in a chapter full of promises of mercy to them ; and is preceded by a " Fear not ! " There were obstacles to the Lord's glory in that day, and they have increased since then ; but the great shaking will bring them all to the ground. There are obstacles in heaven from evil spirits : but " the powers of heaven shall be shaken," and Satan and his angels cast into earth : Rev. xii ; Matt. xxiv. And Babylon, and the cities of the Gentiles that have exalted themselves against Israel and oppressed it, shall be thrown down in ruins by that mighty earthquake, whose last throe is exhibited in Rev. xvi.

But, as this portion of the text is universally misunderstood by commentators, it will be well to cite the other passages, which foretell the shaking of earth and heaven ; and to show that they stand connected, as these passages do, with mercy to Israel, and the kingdom of Christ.

1. Let us first take Isa. xiii,* xiv.

These chapters describe the day of the Lord : a day, not of mercy, but of wrath, a day wherein God will lay the earth† desolate, and destroy sinners out of it. The inhabitants of it shall be burned, and few left. The sun, moon and stars shall be smitten. "*Therefore I will shake the heavens, and the earth shall be removed out of her place,* in the wrath of the Lord of hosts, and in the day of his fierce anger." Babylon shall become desolate. But there shall be mercy on Jacob, and restoration to his own land, with power over those that once oppressed him. *The Lord shall give* REST. Then follows the dirge over their Great Kingly Oppressor.

2. Take again, Isa. xxiv, xxv.

The great and terrible day of the Lord, in its effects upon the whole earth, is described. The windows of heaven are opened, the earth shakes. The powers of heaven are cast down and punished, and the kings of earth. "Then the moon shall be confounded, and the sun ashamed, when *the Lord of Hosts shall reign in Mount Zion* and in Jerusalem, and before his ancients gloriously." Thereupon follows the song of triumph, celebrating the swallowing up of death in resurrection, and the removal of the vail from off the hearts of the nations.

3. Of the same act of shaking, Joel twice speaks. He

---

* 2 Sam. xxii, 8, and the adjacent verses, speak of the shaking of heaven and earth, and of the resurrection of the saints of Israel. But as Psalm xviii, which is identical, does not, in the verse named, read " heaven," but " mountains," I look on the passage in Samuel as an error of transcribers, and rest nothing on it.

† Not " land."

describes the coming of the Day of the Lord. It is a day of cloud, and alarm. The locusts come to avenge God. (Compare Rev. ix). "*The earth shall quake before them, the heavens shall tremble,* the sun and the moon shall be dark, and the stars shall withdraw their shining. *And the Lord shall utter his voice* before his army." His day is very terrible—Repent! To this call Israel listens, and then comes the promise of mercy, "Fear not, O land (earth) be glad and rejoice, for the Lord will do great things." The Lord will dwell among them, the Spirit shall be poured out on all flesh. There shall be deliverance in Mount Zion and in Jerusalem.

4. The third chapter exhibits the great confederacy of the Gentiles against Israel, and God's judgments on them. "*The Lord also shall roar out of Zion, and utter his voice from Jerusalem, and the heavens and the earth shall shake, but the Lord shall be the hope of his people, and the strength of the children of Israel. So shall ye know, that I am the Lord your God dwelling in Zion my holy mountain: then shall Jerusalem be holy, and there shall no strangers pass through her any more.*" Here the voice of the Lord is in immediate connection with the shaking of the heavens and the earth, and the prophecy ends with a bright picture of the prosperity of Israel under Messiah's future reign of glory.

In Rev. vi, we have the great shaking;* the heaven is like a fig tree shook by a storm, the stars like unripe figs cast from its boughs; earth too is shaken, mountains and islands are heaved from their places, and men are terrified. It is the prelude to the announcement of the kingdom of the world becoming Christ's, and to mercy returning to "the beloved city," under the thrones set for the saints: Rev. xi; xx, 4.

Thus, then, as the first voice and its shaking of earth were connected with the first covenant with Israel; so

---

* Σεισμος. It should be rendered the "shaking," not "earthquake," for heaven as well as earth is shaken.

the future voice and the future shaking of heaven and
earth are connected with the future covenant to be made
" with the house of Israel and with the house of Judah " ·
Heb. viii, 8.

It is promised by Haggai, as the sequel to the shaking
of heaven and earth, that Messiah shall come, and his
kingdom. Now this was the hope offered by Isaiah, in
the passage first cited from that prophet. In Isaiah
xxxv, is the command to strengthen the weak hands,
because the Lord is coming with recompense, and to
save his people. But the preceding chapter is a view
of that great and terrible Day of the Lord, the destruction of the armies of all earth, the shaking of the heavenly
bodies, and the destruction of the enemies of the Lord
in the land of Edom. That ended, the wilderness shall
be glad, the desert abound with water, the lame shall
leap as an hart.

I have been the more careful to found this on Scripture, because commentators in general have defaced
and destroyed the argument of the apostle. They make
the heavens and the earth to mean the Jewish dispensation ; and the voice that shakes them to have been already
uttered. They assert that the present dispensation of
the Gospel is ever to abide ; an assertion quite opposed
to the teaching of the passage. For we are taught to be
looking for the return of Christ as high-priest of the good
things to come, as lord of " the age to come," of " the
future habitable earth " : (ii, 15), and of " the future
city " (xiii, 24).

A part of the promise given by Haggai is simple, and
easy to be understood ; the apostle therefore expounds
only a portion of it. He would have us remark the force
of the words, " Yet once more." They imply that one
shaking had already taken place, and that another and
a final one had yet to take place, preparatory to the removal of the things shaken. The promise too is to be

taken in connection with another in Isaiah lxvi, to which allusion is presently made. God is about to shake heaven and earth. He is about also to *make* a heaven and earth that shall *remain.* Therefore the old are not to be shaken only, but to be destroyed. The first shaking, apparently, is that on Sinai. Earth only was shaken then. The second shaking is yet future. It is to affect heaven and earth, in order to introduce the kingdom of Christ. For the *shaking* of heaven and earth is not the *removal* of heaven and earth, though all writers, so far as I am aware, have taken it for granted that they are the same.

Now, as the shock of an earthquake makes houses totter, and is apt to produce rents and dislocations, which ultimately compel them to be taken down, so the two shakings of heaven and earth give token of their final dissolution. The apostle argues concerning the former covenant, that God's speaking of another as a " *new* " covenant, made the first the " *old* " covenant ; which word hinted its decay and final removal. So with " the heavens and the earth that are now." Of them too it is said that they shall grow old, be changed, and perish. And the shaking of them is an intimation of their ultimate destruction. As two shocks of paralysis are in general, followed by a third and fatal one, so the heavens and the earth that now exist, are to be dissolved. No place shall be found for them. This also is the testimony of Revelation. As it exhibits to us the shaking of heaven and earth preparatorv to Messiah's kingdom of the thousand years, so it represents to us the removal of the old heavens and earth, at the close of that temporary kingdom. " I saw *a new heaven and earth ;* for the *first heaven and earth was passed away ;* and there was no more sea " : Rev. xxi, 1 ; also xx, 2.

This then is just in character with the argument ot the whole epistle. The apostle is labouring to prove, that all belonging to the old economy, whether its priest-

hood, covenant, ordinances, or temple, were merely temporary. Now he extends the assertion still more widely.
The very earth and heavens which witnessed the framing
of the old covenant, are as temporary as the covenant
itself. This was intimated by the shaking of the Mount
whence the law was given. That first palsy-stroke gave
token of the final dissolution of the heavens and earth.

"As of things that have been created." The force
of this brief clause lies in the perfect tense of its participle.
The apostle would lead our thoughts to two different
creations ; the one, a past, the other a future one. The
final removal of the old heavens and earth will be in pur-
suance of the promise of God, granted, even under the
old dispensation. Isaiah had been commissioned in
two passages, to foretell " new heavens and a new earth,"
which would succeed these. On these the apostle's next
word of inference is founded. "For behold *I create new*
heavens and a *new earth* ; and the former shall not be
remembered, nor come into mind " : Isa. lxv, 17. And
again, "For as the *new heavens and the new earth which*
I WILL MAKE shall REMAIN before me, saith the Lord,
so shall your seed and your name remain " : Isa. lxvi, 22.
From these words it is evident, that the old earth and
heaven are opposed to the new, as things *already made*,
to those which *are to be made*. Hence God says, " the
new heavens and the new earth which *I will make*," as
contrasted with those already in existence. When therefore Jehovah promises that Israel shall abide, as surely
as the *new* heavens and earth, he hints that the *old* heavens
and earth shall *not abide*. The apostle next comments
on the words of Isaiah, "As the new heavens and new
earth which I will make, *shall remain* before me " This
he says proves that the new creation is unlike the old,
in its abiding for ever. It is not one of the things to be
shaken at the advent of Christ, for it will not then be
created. As created *after* the predicted shaking, it is not

to be shaken; and much less to be dissolved. Accordantly herewith, after the destruction of the old heaven and earth, the Most High says, "Behold *I make all things new*" *:* and then, the new Jerusalem of which Paul makes mention here, is shown to John by the attendant angel. That is the circle within which all the things whereunto we are come, will be permanently gathered.

But does this not prove also that the tabernacle in heaven in which Jesus now ministers, will be shaken at the Saviour's second advent; and, therefore, that it will be dissolved? It seems to have been with an eye to such an inference, that the Holy Spirit has inserted a caution against it, Heb. ix, 11, "But Messiah having come, high priest of the future good things, through the greater and more perfect tabernacle not made with hands (that is, *not of this creation*), and not with blood of goats and calves, but with his own blood, entered in once for all into the Holiest, having obtained eternal redemption." As then the tabernacle and its holiest in heaven are not accounted as belonging to the heaven and earth of the prophet; as they belong indeed to another system and creation; they are not to be shaken at Christ's advent, nor dissolved. But it is very observable that the temple in heaven, which makes so conspicuous a figure in Revelation up to the time of the Saviour's second coming, is beheld no more after it. In the new and final city of the just, John tells us that he saw *no* temple : Rev. xxi, 22.

28. "Wherefore, let us, receiving a kingdom not shaken, hold fast grace,* by which we may serve God acceptably with reverence and godly fear. 29. For our God is a consuming fire."

The abruptness of the apostle's argumentation renders it very difficult to catch the connection. But the reason of his brevity is also apparent. He counted on the perfect familiarity of *Jews* with the writings of the

* So the margin.

Old Testament. He knew that a single word would be sufficient to recall to their minds the treasured prophecies which related to Messiah's kingdom of glory.

In the verse before us, there is first an assumption, and then an exhortation founded thereon. (1) Paul assumes that the saints receive a kingdom not to be shaken at the time of the concussion of heaven and earth. This assumption is based on two passages of the prophets. Its unshaken and eternal character is seen in the promise by Daniel. "The saints of the Most High* shall *take the kingdom, and possess the kingdom, for ever, and for ever and ever" :* Dan. vii, 18. But their eternity of possession is contrasted with the kingdoms of earth, and the shaking of the earthly by the words " not shaken," applying to the heavenly. The apostle is referring to the second passage in Haggai, which foretells the shaking of heaven and earth. " I will shake the heaven and the earth, and I will *overthrow* the throne of *kingdoms,* and *I will destroy* the strength of *the kingdoms of the Gentiles :"* Hag. ii, 21, 22. Here then are the *shaken kingdoms of the earth,* as well as the shaken earth. But our kingdom is not earthly, and so is unshaken and eternal. This kingdom we are to receive* by promise of God, at our entrance upon eternal life, after the destruction of the old heavens and earth.

But a kingdom that will be shaken precedes the eternal and unshaken one. The kingdom must yet be given to Israel, according to the promise. " And thou, oh tower of the flock, *the stronghold of the daughter of Zion, to thee it shall come, even the first dominion : the kingdom shall come to the daughter of Jerusalem" :* Mic. iv, 8. The Saviour recognises it, in his reply to the inquiry of the apostles. They ask, after his resurrection, whether it was then to appear ? He rebukes them indeed for wishing

---

* Paul uses the very verb employed by the Greek version. Παραλαμ-βανοντες. Παραληψονται την βασιλειαν ἁγιοι Ὑψιστου.

to know the period, when he had declared that the times and seasons of these future scenes are kept by the Father in his own hand ; but his words recognize the reality of this Jewish expectation : Acts i, 6, 7. Matt. xxiv, 36.

Among the shaken thrones of kingdoms will be that of Israel ; and the sceptre will be transferred from the hand of the false Messiah then wielding it, to the hand of the true Messiah. As the first shaking of earth at Sinai introduced Israel into the land under covenant, and the kingdom of David and Solomon followed ; so, after the second shaking of heaven and earth, will Israel be afresh restored to their land, under the better covenant ; and the kingdom of the Son of David will be set up. At his future coming in the clouds of heaven, the Spirit by Daniel promises him a dominion over earth and its inhabitants : Dan. vii. Yes ; he is to govern the same earth over which the four former monarchies have ruled. Then will Jesus appear as Melchisedec the priest-king, blessing Israel, on their return from the slaughter of the Gentile kings. His reign will be over the shaken heaven, as well as over the shaken earth.

For the kingdom of Messiah is, as it were, the fruit of the law. The glory of the reigns of David and Solomon, was the blossom, giving token and promise of the ripened fruit. Jehovah, at the giving of the law, offered a kingdom to Israel as the result of their obedience. " Now therefore, if ye will obey my voice indeed, and keep my covenant then ye shall be unto me a peculiar treasure above all people ; for all the earth is mine. And ye shall be unto me a *kingdom of priests* and an holy nation " : Exod. xix, 5, 6. This kingdom they could not obtain by the fulfilment of the condition. It is, however, obtained for them at length by Messiah's obedience. It is the result of the promises to the Son of David. For no jot or tittle can fall from the law, till all be fulfilled. " The days of heaven on earth " will then be accomplished. Jerusalem will be " the city of the Great King." But " the servant (slave) abides not in the house for ever." The promises of the Law are but temporary. " We have *here* no *continuing* city," and the glory of Jerusalem is but for a thousand years. It will be shaken at the coming of Christ, and so, it would appear, will pass away like the rest of the earth : Zech. xiv, 4, 5.

But our Jerusalem and our Mount Zion are not temporary. " We are seeking the one (city) to come." Hence, while the shaken kingdom and its metropolis pass away after the millennium, ours abide. The kingdom of the Son of *David*, so far as it rests on an earthly basis, and is connected with the old covenant, departs ; but the kingdom of the Son of *God*, and the new covenant, abide. Their kingdom was rested on the basis of works, and that is not a lasting foundation. But ours is fastened to grace ; and the issue is eternal life, and a kingdom never to pass away.

As truly as the earth, and the city of the new covenant abide, so shall the kingdom. Hence, after the thousand years of the reign with Messiah in Rev. xx, we read Rev. xxii, 5, " And they shall *reign for ever and ever*." We may see also intimations of the two in the first chapter of the epistle. The apostle in the eighth and ninth verses quotes a passage from the xlvth Psalm descriptive of the millennial reign : but the next quotation gives us Messiah's removal of the old earth, himself remaining the same.* The hopes of the law, as conversant with objects of sense, are not eternal ; but ours are everlasting, as conversant with the things unseen : 2 Cor. iv, 18.

There are then two losses possible, each of which is

* Is this double reign intimated in the remarkable twofoldness of expression in Dan. vii, 18 ? May the saints ' *taking* the kingdom עד עלמא refer to the millennial reign, and their *possessing* it *for ever and ever*,' refer to " the everlasting covenant " on the new earth ?

treated of in its turn. The saint may fall from the favour
of God by misconduct, which will involve loss like Esau's,
and the exclusion from the kingdom of the thousand
years : though, he fail not of salvation altogether and
finally.

But it is threatened to the believer who shall wholly
apostatize from Christ, that he shall fall from eternal
life to everlasting wrath and death. This is the threat
implied in the last example, and would involve the loss
of the *eternal* kingdom of God.

The danger of the lame being turned out of the way
indicates the tendencies to apostasy. Therefore the
example of Israel, and the threats against those who
follow another god, and fall away from grace to justice
fitly come in, verses 12, 13.

"Let us hold fast grace." The old covenant is justice, and the new covenant is grace. The temptation *then*
held before the eyes of the Hebrew Christians was, to
desert the gospel and its grace, for the law and its justice ; in order to escape the persecutions of their countrymen. But that is to find God a fire, as he appeared
on Sinai. Paul therefore exhorts them, not to leave
the Mediator and his blood, with its voice of mercy.

The apostle appropriately connects our holding fast of
grace with the *eternal* kingdom. For into that we enter
solely as the free gift of God on faith in his Son : as our
entrance into the temporary kingdom of Messiah is made
dependent on our works.

"By which we may serve God acceptably." Under
the new covenant God is able to *give* you that aid, both
in understanding and affections, which the law and its
just demands could not. Hence God in the *spiritual*
part of the new covenant, which already takes effect,
says—"I will put my laws into their hearts." "All
shall know me." "Their sins and iniquities I will remember no more." The Holy Ghost takes his title, in this

epistle, from this foundation principle of the new covenant. He is " the Spirit *of grace.*"

There was a competing service of God, which was the favourite one, in Paul's day. It was the outward and shadowy service of the law. But it was no longer acceptable to God. Though once arranged and commanded of God, it was deadly now to any who fell away from Christ to observe it. For even in its day of authority, it derived all its glory and acceptableness from what it shadowed of the Christ. To leave then Christ and the Spirit of grace, in order to turn back to the empty elements, was deeply affronting to God.

" With reference and godly fear." These words teach the temper of the service now to be rendered to God. " Reverence " or awe is required : the opposite to those high and foolish thoughts of our goodness, our works and our deserts, which are so natural to man. The sense of God's supreme majesty and holiness with an eye turned on our own weakness, insignificance, and dependence, and the thoughts of appearing before him in judgment, may well work in us awe.

" And godly fear." This seems to respect God as the God of justice. That attribute he still retains, though the dispensation be of mercy. A sense of the blessedness of our standing in grace, and of our destruction if dealt with by justice, must ever work in us godly fear. As God is awful in his power to destroy, so must we cultivate ever a holy fear of him. Some indeed point to the passage, " Perfect love casteth out fear ; because fear hath torment." But our love ever wants many degrees of perfection ; and, till then, fear is an acceptable and a necessary element of true worship. Grace will then teach us that abiding fear, which is the opposite to the profaneness of Esau. It will instruct us ever to feel and to manifest that reverential spirit, which all the examples of God's justice on offenders in the desert, failed to impress abidingly on Israel.

" For our God is a consuming fire."* The scriptural
picture of the perfections of the Godhead is one never
sketched by man. It combines seemingly contradictory
attributes—perfect justice, with perfect mercy. Even
now that it is discovered to us, many do not understand
it, many refuse it as not the true exhibition of God. It
was probably a perception of the seeming irreconcileability
of these perfections that emboldened the Gnostics to
attempt to sever the God of the Old Testament from the
God of the New. But the believer must accept both
views of God. " God is *love*." " Our God is a consuming
fire." As perfect in mercy, he is the *Father*. As perfect
in justice, he is the consuming fire.

Be it observed that the apostle drops a part of the title
of the Most High as given in Deuteronomy. There it is,
" *The Lord* thy God is a consuming fire." But that is the
Jewish title of the Most High, and therefore unsuitable
here.

God showed himself as the fire on Mount Sinai. He
spake his commands out of fire. The sight of his glory
on the Mount when the covenant was accepted, was like
devouring fire. We must be standing, either at Mount
Sinai under God the just, or at Mount Zion the heavenly
under the God of all grace.

God therefore is to all who desert grace a consuming
fire. This is the warning to those who turn from the
Mediator and his blood. They will be as fuel fully dry.
Fiery indignation will consume them as " adversaries."
Thus then the example of Esau shows God's firmness
as a Father, to those saints who transgress, but still acknowledge Jesus and his grace. But Sinai is the warning, to
all those who apostatize from the grace of the new covenant
to the justice of the old.

---

* Does not the καὶ γαρ express more than the simple γαρ ? Is
it not—' for—also ? ' God has been spoken of before, as a
Father.

The force of this solemn passage in its bearing on the saint has long been destroyed, by denying that it refers to him. To " fail of the grace of God," according to Owen, is not to fall from grace, but not to obtain it, though apparently on the way to it. The contrary is evident from the passage itself. Verses five to eleven are a direct assumption that the parties addressed were *sons of God*, and the conduct befitting sons is enforced on them, as arising out of the relationship. Even the lame who were in danger of being turned out of the way are supposed to be in it up to that time. The persons described as in danger of apostasy, in the sixth chapter, are true believers. And if we look at the illustration employed to discover to us the future issues of our conduct, the proof is corroborated. Esau was a *son*, and, to the last, not apostate. He was *in possession of the birthright*, else he could not have sold it. This therefore cannot correspond with the case of those who are destitute of grace, but to theirs who are in actual possession of it.

The whole of the passage then is designed to impress on the believer the deep necessity of holiness. God has at various times manifested himself in diverse manners, but his holiness abides the same. He spoke in one way under the law, in another under the Gospel ; but in every dispensation alike holiness is demanded. It arises from the very essence of the divine nature. " I will be sanctified in them that come nigh me," must ever be true. " *Be ye holy, for I am holy*," manifests the necessary connection between the character of the worshipper, and of the God he worships " Without holiness *none* " of any dispensation " shall see the Lord."

But the just demand of sanctification by God may be met by failure to render it on our part. If we feel not the need of it now, we shall—when, as Isaiah, we are set face to face before the Holy One. But it is certain that many of the regenerate do not live the life of the saint. Some lead lives that stumble the inquirer, and cause the ungodly to blaspheme. Shall such pass joyously the day of account ?

And, while none who will finally be saved throw themselves finally off from grace as the principle of their acceptance with God, yet it is to be feared that very many act deliberately on principles opposed to grace. What is an oath, however solemnly taken, and in a court of justice, but a consenting to put ourselves off from the ground of mercy, to be dealt with by God's justice according as our deeds deserve ? We consent to peril our salvation on the ground of our saying the truth. This then is not holding fast grace, but welcoming justice to be God's principle of dealing with us.

Some Christians rigorously exact their debts ; some will not forgive an insult or injury. Can such saints behold the Lord's face in grace ? Saith he not, " With the same measure that ye mete withal, it shall be measured to you again ? " And if we make justice the rule of our intercourse with others, this will be brought to bear on ourselves in the day of the Lord. Is not this the very teaching of the parable of the unmerciful servant ? Matt. xviii.

Let us then give things temporal in exchange for things eternal ; for this is the barter of faith, and will reward us with joy in the day of the Lord. But to exchange the kingdom for the unstable, unsatisfying things of sense, will cause us bitter and unavailing sorrow, in the hour of recompense before our Master.

And perceiving how greatly we have failed, and how bright and spotless the purity of Him to whom we shall have to render in our account, may we ever be lowly, ever be fearful to offend ! Let us know and believe the love that God hath to us, that we may love him in return ! But let us also perfect holiness in *the fear of God !*

CHAPTER VI

THE RESPONSIBILITY OF TEACHERS

1 Cor. iii, iv.

In the early part of the epistle to the Corinthians, the apostle had considered it his duty to rebuke the parties existing in that church. Those parties took their rise from natural predilections for some especial ministers of Christ. But the formation of such factions was wholly alien to the gospel. The doctrine of a crucified Messiah, disdained the addition of human wisdom. It was God's purpose in the present dispensation, to make the primary truths of the gospel distasteful to the worldly-wise, whether among the Jews or the Gentiles. The Jews looked for *power,* and were repelled by the sight of a Messiah executed in weakness. The Gentiles demanded profound *philosophy,* and were repelled by the simple tale of the crucified One of the Jewish nation. Yet God, in spite of it, put forth *his* power beneath that appearance of weakness, and his wisdom beneath that semblance of folly. The Holy Spirit too, poured into the minds of those enlightened by the cross of Messiah, supernatural and unearthly light.

Of that illumination Paul was in full possession. Divine intelligence he gladly imparted to those who were in a fit state of mind for its reception. But to that height of spiritual attainment Corinthian believers had not yet reached. Their discords and partizanships were the full proof of the apostle's estimate of their low spiritual state.

4. " For while one is saying, I am of Paul, and another, I am of Apollos, are ye not carnal ? 5. Who then is Paul, and who is Apollos ? but ministers by whom ye believed ? and unto each as the Lord gave."*

This brings us to the especial subject that is now to employ us. The words before us regard the estimation in which *ministers* of Christ are to be held. The Corinthians had made them heads of parties. But that was to set them in a position wholly unsuitable to them. They were but servants of one Lord. They were only means and instruments to bring men to faith in the Saviour, and acquaintance with his will. Let them therefore recognize the servant in his place, and the Master in his.

The last clause of the verse presents a difficulty. Our translators have got over it by altering the position of the words. But this does not seem the way in which the apostle would have expressed himself, had his meaning been that which our translation gives. There was no manner of use in inserting the " even." The conjunction shows, that a new clause is added. Something then must be expressed to fill up the ellipsis. But what should be inserted, is not clear. It should be, however, I believe, one of the two following supplements :—

" Ministers by whom ye believed."

1. " And (*ye believed*) each, as the Lord gave."

Or we must supply " ministers " from the preceding context.

" Ministers by whom ye believed."

" And (ministers) unto each, as the Lord gave."

The sentiment in either case will be, that not only is the salvation of each saint a matter of God's decree, but that

* Και εκαστω ως ο Κυριος εδωκεν. Some critical editions omit the ' but ' before ' ministers.'

the means and ministry by which it is to be effected, are also of his ordination. This is an important truth. The Saviour decides, by whom, as his evangelists, each soul is to be converted.

It was then by no original energy, and no independent powers of Paul or Apollos, that they made converts to the faith of Christ. Those who believed beneath their word were given to them.

6. " I planted, Apollos watered, but God gave the increase."

The relative importance of the ministry of Paul and Apollos is represented to us under the figure of the toil of the husbandman, or planter. Paul's work was the first, the most laborious, and important. He had to dig the soil, and to set the vines. Apollos came after to supply the water needed. The labour was important, but secondary. He advanced in knowledge those already added to the faith of Christ.

But next, both these agencies are compared with that of God.

7. " So then neither is he that planteth any thing, neither he that watereth, but God that giveth the increase."

Both planting and watering are but external ministries ; both would be in vain, were there not an inward agency at work, to give efficiency to them both. The glory then should be his, to whom belongs what is inward and essential in the matter ; not theirs, who are engaged only about the means. All the labour of Paul and Apollos had been in vain, but for the grace of the Most High.

8. " Now he that planteth and he that watereth are one ; but each shall receive his own reward according to his own labour."

Not only are ministers nothing in respect of the Master that employs them, and to whom alone their powers and their successes are owing; but they are members of one body, moving in one work, designing one end by harmonious means. The unity then which God loves among his workmen is not to be broken, by Christians seeking to sever them into parties and sections.

A remarkable sentiment follows, in seeming contradiction to that just preceding. If all ministers are one, surely they will be equally rewarded! No! individual action will come into question at the close. They may work unitedly now, but in the reckoning before Christ, each will give an account of himself individually. "Let each prove his own work, and then shall he have rejoicing unto himself alone, and not unto another. *For each shall bear his own burthen*" · Gal. vi, 4, 5.

The insertion of the word "man," in this passage, and in the one in Galatians, disfigures the sense. Paul is speaking, not of *men* in general, nor ever of Christians generally, but of Christian teachers.

"Each shall receive his own reward." Most important truth! It asserts not only degrees of reward, but peculiarities of reward. None will be able, righteously, to exchange his reward with any other. The labours of no two are alike. Neither then shall the rewards be equal. The teacher—other things being equal—shall receive greater reward than the hearer; as his responsibility and labour are greater. But not only so. One teacher shall take his station in glory in advance of another teacher. The principle of reward will be that of justice: "according to works." It will not be according to *dignity*, or estimation among men. Exaltation among men, and even among Christians, often leads to ministers falling off in zeal and labour. But labour is to be the ground of reward before God; and this applies equally to the several forms of it. It is to be *labour* again, that is to be the basis of adjudication, not *success*. For success is not in our power, though the want of it should create suspicions in Christian ministers, that all is not right in themselves, or in their position.

9. " For we are God's fellow-labourers, ye are God's husbandry, God's building."

Two meanings may be given to the first sentiment. **(1)** That Christian ministers are co-operating with God in the production of a common end. It is a beautiful and ennobling thought. That is the view which our translators evidently took of the passage. But I do not think that it is the correct one. It appears to me, that such a construction would have required " God " to be in the dative ; not in the genitive, as here. Also the two following clauses, in which the same construction holds, satisfy me that the sense is rather as follows :—(2) " I, and Apollos, and Peter, are *fellow-labourers who belong to God ;* you are a field and building belonging to him. As we all, whether teacher or taught, belong to God, you are not to take our names, as though you belonged to us. And we, as fellow-labourers of the same master, are not to be forced apart from one another, as leaders of factions."

The house does not belong to the bricklayer, nor the field to the ploughman. You are *God's* husbandry, *God's* building. Beautifully does the apostle here unite two metaphors. He had before represented his own work and that of Apollos, as that of farm-servants. He now employs the figure of a building, to bring into view a new truth.

The previous figure had exhibited the nothingness of human agency in comparison of Divine. But the present metaphor inculcates *the responsibility of the Christian minister to God.*

10. " According to the grace of God which is given to me, as a wise architect, I have laid the foundation, but another is building on it. But let each take heed how he buildeth on it."

Paul, in this verse, takes to himself the character of a " *wise* architect." But, ere he thus describes himself, he is careful to give to God the praise of his wisdom. He is wise, by wisdom given from on high. Let God ever have his due !

In the figures employed, he still maintains his comparative superiority, to any teacher of the Corinthian church who might succeed him. As, before, he described himself as the planter, so, now, as the layer of the foundation of the house. This is the most laborious part of the building, and therefore that which claims the most regard, if done well. Without Paul's previous labour, there had been no place for the superstructure of Apollos.

But the Lord had called Paul to labour elsewhere, for it was his office to raise churches for the Saviour. Another had taken his post, and was raising the superstructure. Not all are teachers. Nor does it become the Christian minister ever to be laying the foundation. *That* once well laid, the superstructure is to be raised. The saints are to be led on to the full knowledge of Christ, to the deeper things of God.

But while the further edification of the saints was a matter of duty and of necessity, it was no less full of responsibility to the teacher. Observe, that the *builder* is addressed. " Let each (not ' every *man*,' but ' teacher,' understood) take heed how he buildeth thereupon." It is a lesson ever needed. Yet the account to be rendered by the believing minister, of the doctrines he has preached, is a subject seldom or never treated of.

The general impression seems to be, that all that can legitimately be demanded, is the preaching of the truth that saves—the great fundamentals of justification, and sanctification. But the apostle's caution is entered, not in regard to those foundation and vital truths, but to the *subordinate* doctrines of the faith. The " take heed," refers to the superstructure. " Let each take heed, how he *buildeth upon* " *the foundation.*

11. " For other foundation can none lay, beside what is laid which is Jesus (is) the Christ."

The apostle's work could not be superseded by any one who came after him. The foundations of the faith must be the same everywhere. All Christian teachers who succeeded him must take for granted the great fundamentals which Paul had inculcated.

But the superstructure might be different in different churches. There is a great copiousness and variety in the subordinate truths of the Christian faith, flowing from the great sources. And the circumstances of different churches, as well as the range of knowledge in different teachers, would naturally give a prominence in some cases to certain truths. How different the characters of Paul's Epistles to different churches! Their difficulties, dangers, and degree of advancement drew forth from the riches of the apostle's wisdom, the topics most required.

The present verse decides a question which is afterwards raised, concerning the nature of the *materials* supposed to be used.

1. Some suppose that *persons* are the materials in the eye of the apostle. 2. Others, that *doctrines* are intended.

But the foundation which Paul laid at Corinth was the *doctrine* concerning Christ. Over Christ's *person* he had no power. He did not introduce him personally to the church. He had only to declare the truths concerning him. By parity of reason then, the superstructure is of the same kind as the foundation ; and as the foundation is a doctrine, or set of doctrines, so is the superstructure.

2. Nor does it appear that Christian ministers are responsible for introducing to the church none but true believers. If it be their aim to receive those only who give credible evidence of being born again ; this is all that can be required. We read of no rebuke administered to Philip for accepting Simon Magus. Nor does Paul esteem himself or any other in fault for admitting to church fellowship,

those who afterwards fell away to blasphemy or immorality. And indeed, as far as regards the churches of believers in this country, they are generally received, not on the judgment, or by the instrumentality of one, but by the general vote and decision of the whole. It does not therefore appear, that the question relates to the reception of believers or unbelievers, but regards the preaching of doctrines ; over which the teacher has entire control, and therefore in regard to which he is thoroughly responsible.

Jesus alone is the foundation of the church. None but the God-man can bear the weight of salvation rested on him. He only can make atonement : he only intercede on high. His past and present work, is the resting-place of the soul. His future work defined by the word of prophecy, is the groundwork of hope. At his coming, the toils of the way will be over.

12. " But if any build upon this foundation, gold, silver, precious stones, wood, hay, stubble : 13. The work of each shall become manifest : for the day shall declare it : for it is revealed in fire ; and the fire shall try the work of each, of what sort it is."

The materials which may be built upon this precious corner-stone of the faith, are of two kinds ; arranged in reference to the test of fire which is to be afterwards applied to them. The three first are materials not liable to be consumed ; the three last, are easily inflammable. Now as fire is to try the work of each, it must be of deep importance to each builder to employ only those which are incombustible.

Thus, by means of a figure, the apostle gives us to understand, that Christian teachers may lay before the saints either the truths of God, or the doctrines of men. The truths of God will stand the test of the coming day of account. The doctrines of men will not.

But the doctrines of men again may be described as aking two main currents. (1) The preacher may insist on adding to the Word of God, the *traditions* of the visible church. He may descant on the beauty and necessity of rites and ceremonies appointed by " the church," that is, by *men*. His teaching may be of feasts and fasts, of articles, councils, the fathers, and the necessary submission of the judgment to the authority of men. (2) Or his mind may be of an opposite turn. He may expatiate on the wonders of *philosophy*, and *reason*. He may lead out the souls of his auditors in metaphysic flights, and teach the doctrines of the philosophy of the day intermingled with Scripture phrases.

There is full permission now to each to build, as seems him good. There is no check, but that administered by conscience, the Scripture, or the hearers. But from the responsibility under which each lies, none can free himself. As each Christian ought to be careful, that he holds the truth, so, much more, ought the teacher of others to be careful that he propounds only what is of God. His work of instruction is unchallenged now ; but it will be strictly scrutinized hereafter, both as to motives and substance, by the Great Head of the Church. The trial of the doctrine of each minister of Christ shall be public.

" For the day shall declare it " There is one day which was ever present to the thoughts of the apostle. There is one, to which he would continually turn the gaze of believers. And hence he often speaks of it without specifying it more particularly. Every one in that age could supply the ellipsis. He had already spoken of it before. " Ye come behind," he had said, " in no gift, waiting for *the coming of our Lord Jesus Christ ;* who shall also confirm you to the end, that ye may be blameless *in the day of our Lord Jesus Christ* " : 1 Cor. i, 8. He had required the church to put away the incestuous person, and to deliver him up to Satan, " for the destruction of the flesh, that the spirit may be saved *in the day of our Lord Jesus* " · 1 Cor. v, 5. So, in his second epistle, he said, that his converts were his rejoicing "*in the day of the Lord Jesus.*" He described also the same time more fully in his address to the Romans, as "*the day in which God would judge the secrets of men by Jesus Christ*" : Rom. ɪɪ, 16.

The opinions passed upon doctrine by man, and by each varying age of the Christian church, are no stable foundation on which to rest. The current of opinion and of doctrine varies. The day that is finally to decide what is true and what false, amidst the many styles of doctrine which have been inculcated by various ministers, is that of Jesus. *He* then shall judge, whose decision is perfect. Popularity has often attended false doctrine. It will still more accompany it, as the dark latter days draw on. Then they "will not endure sound doctrine" ; but will choose what pleases. Becoming deaf to the truth, they will be given up to the fables, either ɛf philosophy falsely so called, or to the lying legends of traditions, miracles, and saints.

2. The present is "man's day," the day of his passing sentence, and of his self-exaltation. But the apostle, in the next chapter, leads us to look to the coming of Christ, as the time of real judgment, and of praise for the true servant of Jesus. 3. The day now intended is the day of "reward," as the next verse proves. But the day of reward for the servants of God is not till the sounding of the seventh trump. Then, "the reward" long promised, is to be given : Rev. xi, 15–18.

"For it is revealed in fire."

Thus it is spoken of the day of Christ. "Who may abide *the day of his coming?* And who shall stand, when he appeareth. For he is like *refiner's fire*" : Mal. iii, 2. "The same day that Lot went out of Sodom, it *rained fire* and brimstone from heaven, and destroyed them all. Even thus shall it be in *the day* when the Son of Man is revealed " Luke xvii, 29, 30 ; also 2 Thess. i, 8.

Only, be it observed, the fire mentioned in the two last places is literal and material fire, affecting the persons of men. In the passage under consideration, however, as the builders are so only in a figurative sense, and the materials are not literal gold or wood, so neither is the test that is to be applied to them material fire.

Under this metaphor Christ's active scrutiny of the doctrines taught by his ministers, is foretold. " The fire shall try the work of each of what sort it is." Not all doctrines preached even by converted and conscientious men, are true. Some do not " rightly divide " the word of truth ; but confound together all dispensations ; as though what was once commanded or sanctioned of God, must be equally in force at all times. There are workmen who will pass the examination of their ministry with shame. In that day, doctrine much cavilled at and opposed, may receive the approval of Christ ; and doctrines popular and applauded be rejected as untrue, owing their popularity only to that leaven of evil which still cleaves even to the children of God.

1. It is " the *work* " of each, not the *person* of the teacher, that is spoken of as being subjected to fire. 2. It is not a fire now lighted, but a future one, kindled when " the day of the Lord " is come. 3. It is metaphoric, not real ; as has been noted above. These observations evince how vainly Roman Catholics rest their doctrine of purgatory on the passage under consideration. 4. They suppose, too, that the fire of purgatory attacks every Christian ; while this only applies to Christian teachers. 5. The fire of purgatory, as they teach, is designed to purge the souls of the sinful alone. It is the fire of visitation for sins. But this fire is to try the work of the good and bad workman alike. The teaching of Paul and Apollos, no less than that of ministers of the present day, is to be subjected to its power.

14. " If the work of any abide, which he hath built thereupon, he shall receive a reward."

The *work* of the teacher is primarily concerned in the trial by fire. But he himself is greatly interested in the issue of the ordeal, as it is favourable or unfavourable. Hence the two verdicts, and their consequences, are spread before us. Some will have preached only the pure truths of God. On these the fire will descend harmlessly. Their work will stand the test. Christ will esteem such a one, a steward who has proved himself faithful. He will receive a positive recompense. As his responsibility has been greater than that of Christians in general, so will his reward be.

The same principle, in reference to the teachers of the Law of Moses, is announced by our Saviour in the Sermon on the Mount " Think not that I am come to destroy the Law or the prophets." " Whosoever therefore shall break one of these least commandments, and shall teach men so, shall be called least in the kingdom of heaven ; but whosoever shall do and teach them, he shall be called great in the kingdom of heaven " : Matt. v, 17, 19.

15. " If the work of any shall be burned up,* he shall suffer loss : but himself shall be saved, yet so as through fire."†

To exhibit the latter alternative, the figure of the apostle is expanded. We have only to imagine one of the fearful thunderstorms of those hot Eastern climes. A fire-ball strikes the house of each of the two builders. It touches the house of gold and silver, and glances off. There is nothing inflammable there. But again, it strikes the house of him who has constructed his domicile of wood, hay, or stubble. The fire-bolt sets it in flames in a moment. The householder awakes, and finds to his dismay, that his building is consuming over his head.

Such will be the case of one, who, together with the foundation truths of salvation, has preached human traditions ; or the philosophy of the day. He will stand before

* Κατακαησεται.　　　　† Δια πορος.

the presence of Christ ashamed. The contrariety of his teaching to that of the Scripture will be instantly apparent, even to himself. The vain arguments by which he sought to justify it to his own mind and to others, will be dissipated in a moment. Nothing but the Lord's *truth* will stand the *day* of the Lord.

His work is " burned *up.*" From this it would appear, that the two extreme cases are in question : one, where all the teaching has been genuine : one, where all the subordinate instruction has been false.

In such a case the builder " shall suffer loss." The word is more definite in the original than in the translation. It signifies, " he shall be fined." It is ordinarily spoken of penalties in money exacted of offenders. Christ pays to the one teacher recompense. But the other not only receives no payment : he has himself to *make* it. He not only suffers the loss of his work, which is consumed ; but a further fine is inflicted, as punishment. What then is that fine ? It is not that of his *soul*, of which the Saviour once says :—" What is a man profited, if he shall gain the whole world, but (be fined) lose his own soul ? " Matt. xvi, 26. For we are told presently after, that he shall be saved. Can the loss then be any other, than the loss of the millennial kingdom ?

And will not that award be just ? Was it not in his power to know what God's truth is ? Has not the Holy One given us his sacred Book, and promised the teaching of the Holy Spirit to them that seek for it ? The real causes of most, or of *all* false doctrine, are sinful. The eye of the teacher is not single. He will rather teach what is for his present interests, than that which is well pleasing to God. Some are deterred from examining the Word of God by sloth ; some, by the fear of censure, are kept back from proclaiming what they see on its pages ; some, by the perception, that to preach the doctrines there set forth would lead to loss of worldly standing, or of money ; some are guided wholly by human authority, neglecting the divine. But are not these, and similar reasons, worthy of rebuke ?

2. But not only do false doctrines take their rise from sinful feelings in the preacher's mind ; but they end not there. Many wait upon the teacher's lips. Most, without examination, receive what he utters. Hence they too suffer loss. They are guided through life by false principles. And false principles are intimately connected with wrong practice. Consequently the teacher of false doctrines on subordinate points is responsible for the errors of those affected by his teaching. As the truth of God would have nourished and led on the souls of his believing hearers, so have the errors which he has proclaimed stunted their growth, and destroyed their vigour. Shall a baker be responsible for the quality of his flour, and the wholesomeness of his bread ; and shall not the Christian teacher be justly summoned to account to Christ for the doctrines to which he has given currency ?

" But he himself shall be saved." In these few words is contained the force of the passage, as applying to *converted* ministers. The apostle is describing believing teachers in both cases. The very man whose work is consumed, is yet saved at last. We have not to do then with the case of the guide who is utterly blind, and who is leading men blind as himself.

The lot of both there is, as the Saviour declares, the *pit.** The builder here is saved, because he held aright the one great mode of acceptance with God. He led his hearers too, to trust in the one foundation given of God. Hence his salvation is guaranteed. The trial of the text is not that of the ungodly, whose eternal life or death hangs on the decision of the judge. He has by faith passed from death to life.

---

* Βοθυνον. Not ' the ditch.' One might easily get out of that, not so easily out of a pit-fall made to entrap wild beasts.

But his escape is "so as through fire." The rendering, "*by* fire," has wonderfully darkened the meaning of the apostle. It has led the reader to imagine, that the fire *is the means of his salvation;* and therefore that it exerts a purifying agency upon him. But no; the meaning is, that the fire is that enemy through which he has to make his way. His house is on fire, above and around him. He has to burst through the flames, in order to escape from the conflagration.*

That it is not a real fire, is again noticed in the expression, "*so as* through fire." His escape is like the escape of the scorched and terrified householder. He is ashamed of his unfaithfulness. His disgrace is made manifest to angels and the saved. He is shut out with dismay and anguish, from the kingdom.† He feels, that the fault is his own. His fellow enters with joy.

It is evident from this passage as from others, that the Scriptures present to us something more than bare salvation ; and are very far from asserting, that all the saved will be equal. Great indeed the contrast, between the two builders, and their recompenses !

How unsound then is the popular view, which represents the subordinate doctrines of Christianity, as of little importance. " If a minister teach the great fundamentals of the faith, why ask for more ? Never will it be asked in heaven, whether you belonged to the Methodists or to the Establishment ; to the Baptists, or the Independents ! "

---

* A similar error has been committed in regard to 1 Pet. iii, 21. " Eight souls were saved by water." Nay, but " escaped *through* water." The water was their foe. It brought death to all others. Then safety consisted in getting out of its reach. Again, " Who *by* the letter and circumcision dost transgress the law ; " Rom. ii, 27. Nay, but who " *through* the letter." That and circumcision are a double hedge, through which the trespasser breaks.

† This result in the metaphor, answers to the difficulty of the escape from the flaming house. The house is in one view of it consumed ; in another it is on fire, in order to illustrate his position from two points of view.

Nay, but it will ! The subordinate views of every teacher and of each hearer too, will come into question. And reputation, or loss will turn greatly upon the difference of the doctrines held and acted on.

How important then for ministers, both of the Establishment and of Dissenters, to prove all that they teach by God's word : and to found on the New Testament all that they teach, as the duty of a disciple of Christ !   .

Should not the clergyman inquire with solemnity and singleness of eye, whether the Prayer-book does not confound the Law and the Gospel, in many of its services ?   Should he not ask, whether oaths and war are permitted by Jesus ? and whether the union of Church and State, that is, of the world and the church, is according to the mind of his Master ?   Is infant baptism an ordinance of Jesus ?

Should not the Dissenter inquire too, whether the coming of God does not demand the presence of Christ in person ? That, and the post-millennial coming of Christ, cannot both be true.   Does the New Testament urge the Christian to seek to be great in the riches and honours of the world ? Does it encourage him to drink deeply into the philosophy of this present evil age ?   Does it incite him to plunge into politics ?   The doctrine of the verbal inspiration of Scripture, and the modern theory, cannot both be true.   The doctrine of the eternity of the punishment of the wicked, and its non-eternity cannot both be genuine ; which does the Scripture teach ?   Which do you ?   Are the servants of Christ to invite sinners to him, or merely to preach to the elect ?   Both doctrines cannot be Scriptural.   Which does the Scripture affirm ?   One of these will be burnt up as stubble.   Which is it ?

How necessary to poise in God's scales, fellow-workmen in the Gospel, all that we teach !   It is not, what can be said upon a passage of Scripture ; not what will make the most brilliant, learned, poetic, or philosophic sermon, that should be our inquiry.   But, what saith God ?   It is not,

what will bring present favour ? But, what will stand
the eye of Christ ?

We had better be ashamed now, than then. Better
confess our previous errors, when we have discovered them
by the prayerful study of Scripture, than meet the day of
Christ, as one whose work is to be consumed, and whose
escape is to be as through flames.

It is in view of our peculiar responsibility as preachers,
that James enforces his exhortation · " My brethren,
become* not many teachers, knowing that *we shall receive
greater judgment* " : James iii, 1. Jesus expects more from
them than from others, both in doctrine and practice. " Art
thou the teacher† of Israel and know not these things ? "
John iii, 10. " Ye blind guides, which strain out‡ the gnat,
but swallow the camel l "

The principle is just, that they who lead, should be
especially careful that they know the way. They do not
move wrong alone. Their mistakes involve others in like
mischief.

Does not even human government hold the chemist
responsible, if he should dispense arsenic for quinine, or
oxalic acid for Epsom salts ? Is not the surgeon responsible
for his mode of treating disease ? Is it enough, that he
does not kill outright ? Is he not bound to use means
suited to cure ? Is it enough for the baker to plead, that
though his loaves were unwholesome, they did not kill ;
and really contained more wheat-flour than chalk or alum ?

Shall others give account to Christ how they spent their
money and time ; and shall not we be the more called on
to account, how we *taught* them to use their money and
their time ?

Again, can error produce the same holy present results
as truth ? Will chalk and bone-dust sustain the labourer's
strength as well as wheat-meal ? Will they develop as
healthily the frame of the young child ? If we teach others

* Γινεσθε,   † Ο διδασκαλος.   ‡ Διυλιζω.

to think wrongly or to act wrongly, who can say how far the evil consequences extend ? Great as is the blessing of truth, so great is the damage inflicted by error, even though it be error on subordinate points. And who can doubt, that among the regenerate teachers of the faith, there is a vast amount of error taught, on points not destroying ultimate salvation ? There may be some few workmen that will not be ashamed, as rightly dividing the word of truth. But there are very many, ignorant of the difference of dispensations, or wilfully disregarding it, who mass together into one confused conglomerate whatever they find in Scripture. They hurl together into utter chaos, the principles of the law and those of the gospel. But can false doctrine on these points, produce right practice ? Can anything but the pure word of the kingdom draw forth the conduct worthy of the kingdom ?

Error of principle is necessarily associated with erroneous conduct. There may indeed be disobedience where the unadulterated doctrines of the New Testament are proclaimed ; but the teacher in that case is free of blame. The life of the hearer is then in contradiction with the forces brought to bear upon him. But obedience to false doctrines on subordinate points produces a life unsuited to the peculiarities of Christ's precepts, and hinders fruit to the glory of God. Not only so : it shuts up the Scripture in many of its parts, infusing darkness into light, dimming the glory of God's character, and causing discord among those who are fundamentally one in Christ.

Such being the responsibility of those who minister the gospel of God, how diligently, my fellow ministers, should we scrutinize our doctrine ! Each teacher is a householder. The system of truth which he holds and teaches is a house, which he has built for himself. Of what kind then is that building ? Now is the time to inquire ; for now mistake may be rectified. Hereafter it will be too late. Have we tested, by Scripture, the doctrines of which our structure is composed ? Or have we received them in the lump, by tradition ? Have we used, without scruple, and without examination, whatever was accredited among those with whom we associate ? Have we taken for granted, that whatever professors of divinity taught, and our denomination holds, must needs be true ? Are we sure, that every part of our teaching is sound in itself, accordant with, or rather derived from, the New Testament model ? Do we ever remember our responsibility to use the test of Holy Scripture, and try our materials by it ? If we have not, we shall do well to see to it at once. For our place in the glory to come will materially depend upon the character of our doctrine. Do we inquire, in every text we take, not what may be said upon the passage with striking effect, not how our abilities may be most advantageously displayed, or how ingeniously it may be diverted from its original meaning, nor what great names have said about it, but what is the legitimate meaning deducible from the words ?

Is not the superstructure of thousands of Christian ministers imperfect or untrue, because they never regarded themselves as responsible for doctrine ; or, at least, not responsible, beyond teaching the fundamentals of Christianity ? And are not many, who see dimly that they are wrong in points not directly connected with the believer's justification, unwilling to examine, or determined not to do so ; because they fear that the issue would be destructive of the views they teach ? Are not many afraid to propound truths which they see, because they perceive at a glance that it would embroil them with the mass of their friends, or perhaps thrust them altogether from their post ?

Let me then earnestly enforce on every minister of Christ who reads these pages, the apostle's word of caution. *Take heed what you build!* I assume with him, that the reader receives Jesus as his atonement before God; that he takes him for his present Intercessor before the throne, and acknowledges the Holy Spirit as the Great Agent in regeneration. But it is mournfully possible, as facts abundantly testify, to rear upon this foundation a super-structure wholly or partially erroneous. There may be wilful keeping back of truth; there may be conscientious assertion of what is unscriptural; there may be implied sanction of what is confessed to be evil in doctrine.

The lesson of the text is a great means in the hand of God, to raise his ministers above all unworthy motives in the promulgation of doctrine. Remember, preacher, that you are the servant, directly and primarily, of Christ. You are the servant of his people, for his sake, and under his control. Remember that the Saviour's scrutinizing gaze and searching fire will try your work. Ask yourself concerning every doctrine—Will this stand the day of account? Will Jesus applaud me in that day, as having taught his pure truth and his whole truth?

Let us remember, too, that the teaching, both in its substance and in its style, manifests the heart of the teacher. The earnest student of Scripture will come forth freighted with God's word. The hankerer after philosophy will savour of its vanities. He who is ambitious of a name for eloquence will make it apparent to God, and most probably to his hearers also. If our aim be to astonish and to captivate, we shall employ one style. If our desire be to build for eternity and the eye of Christ, we shall exhibit another and a soberer one.

The showy sermon, the popular doctrine, may win the largest congregation now; but will they stand the day of the Lord? Do they even now produce the best results? Who oftenest hit the target? the archer that with eye intent on the mark steadily draws his arrow to the head, regardless of all around, careful only of the mark before him, or he who desires to be accounted an elegant bowman, and who therefore stands in an elegant attitude, and with graceful action shoots high into air?

16. "Know ye not that ye are the temple of God, and the Spirit of God dwelleth in you ? 17. If any defile the temple of God, him shall God defile ; * for the temple of God is holy, which temple ye are."

Each individual Christian is a temple of God : 1 Cor. vi, 19. But the context here would lead one to believe, that the apostle was speaking of the church as constituting a collective temple, in which, at all times, the Holy Spirit dwells. Now not only might curious and worthless, but even defiling doctrine, be taught in it. Nay, viewing the subject more generally still, not only the teachers of the church might defile it ; but the ordinary members might introduce evil practices and stir up strifes. We have an example of defiling doctrine taught by the false prophetess in the church at Thyatira : Rev. iii. We see that even at Corinth, the sin of the incestuous was gloried in by some of the church, and that they defended their eating in the idol's temple, and even fornication itself. Now these things defiled the temple. And God held all such introducers of defilement responsible. If they made his house unclean, he would defile them when the day of glory should come. When their holier fellows rejoiced in the kingdom of God, they should be dishonoured and mourn.

"For the temple of God is holy." The indwelling of God makes the church holy. Reverence therefore must prevent us from making it unworthy of him. Of this the history of God's actions in his earthly and material temple may give us instruction. Nadab and Abihu used strange fire : they are smitten dead at once before him. The irreverent Bethshemites looked into the ark : they are cut off amidst the very joy of its return. Uzzah puts forth his hand to steady it when shaken, and is stricken to the ground. A king enters to minister as a priest, on the forbidden ground of the temple. *His presence defiled the house, and the Lord defiled him by leprosy.* Ever from that day, all men must

* Φθειρει—φθερει. The same word in both cases.

account him unclean. *Yet he did not cease to be an Israelite and a king.* Gehazi, by his lying and covetousness, defaces the glorious testimony to the grace of the God of Israel! And what is the issue? He who was clean, is defiled. " He went out of his presence a leper as white as snow." Even so, it appears that the present threatening is addressed to believers, and does not involve perdition. " There must be heresies (parties) among you, that the approved may be made manifest." How many believers are guilty of creating parties and strifes in the church to which they belong!

18. " Let none deceive himself : if any among you has the reputation of being wise in this age, let him become a fool, that he may become* wise. 19. For the wisdom of this world is foolishness with God, for it is written, ' He taketh the wise in their own craftiness.' 20. And again, ' The Lord knoweth the reasonings of the wise, that they are vain.' "

If any believer, after this warning, will still hold on his way, in spite of the threats of the Most High, the fault is his, not God's. But many will not believe that God can inflict punishment on the wilfully disobedient saint.

The wisdom of the world must be put off by those who wish to be wise before God. For there are two opposing wisdoms, each of which is foolishness to the other. The wisdom of the present age is foolishness with God. Wisdom for Messiah's age and kingdom is foolishness to the men of the world. We must renounce then the wisdom of the world, that we may be wise with God. This therefore is an admonition, not to mingle the philosophy of man with the truths of God. Wood is a fit material for building in human judgment. But if the house is to be tried with fire, it is unsuitable. We must build then only with divine materials, if we would have our work to stand the day of God.

The believer is to become a fool to the worldly, that he may become really wise. The true doctrine of Christ will

* Γενηται.

ever seem foolish to the world. Reputation therefore for wisdom must be sacrificed. But here lies the difficulty. Few are willing to give up a doctrine they have once asserted, especially if the confession of previous error, and the assertion of the opposite doctrine, will strip them of their repute for understanding and consistency. But all things are better than loss before God.

That the world's wisdom is folly with God, is established by two quotations from the Old Testament. The cleverness of the worldly wise, far from delivering them *from* God, delivers them *up* to God.

There are difficulties connected with both these quotations which as I cannot solve, so I will not raise.

21. "Therefore let none boast in men, for all things are yours. 22. Whether Paul or Apollos, whether Cephas, or the world, whether life or death, whether things present or things to come, all are yours. 23. And ye are Christ's, and Christ is God's."

The party-making spirit of Corinth again receives its rebuke. It was a boasting of men, and a consequent splitting asunder, while a perception of their true position, as servants of the one Master—God—would have united them. What belonged to the ministers, as men, was only worthless : all that was really valuable in each was derived from the One Divine source. The Jews might form themselves into parties headed by human leaders, in their additions to the law. This was the sinfulness of man. The heathen might range themselves into schools of philosophy. This was natural enough to those blinded by unbelief. But Christians were not thus to act.

Paul specifies three of the ministers who were singled out as heads of parties. He bids them cease from this procedure. By overvaluing some, they set themselves against others, and despised valuable powers and means of edification, which God had bestowed upon his ministers, for their service. Paul, and Apollos, and Peter, were all sent

by God for usefulness to his church. And *he* inflicted loss
upon himself, who, by over-estimating one of these, refused
the light and blessing to be obtained from the others. Each
of these servants of God was meant for his benefit, and each
in turn had something to communicate.

But the apostle carries the sentiment a step further. All
things, even Christ himself, belonged to God. He is the
one head to which all things are to be traced up. Here
is the final unity in which the believer may joyfully rest.

IV. 1. " Let a man so account of us, as servants of Christ,
and stewards of the mysteries of God. 2. Moreover, it is required
of stewards, that one be found faithful."

The truth thus announced is of the deepest importance.
The Holy Spirit in the former chapter had rebuked the false
position in which the Corinthian believers had placed the
ministers of the new covenant. But it now takes up the
positive side of the question, and shows in what light they
are to be regarded by those who would view the matter as
it appears to God.

They are " servants of Christ, stewards of God's mysteries." While all believers are in a general sense " servants
of Messiah," these are so in a special sense. Some he has
set to rule his household, to give to each his portion of food
in season. They in a measure act the part which Christ
would have done, had he been on earth. They explain
his will to believers ; they deliver his call to those without.

As servants of Messiah, they are ever to keep themselves,
and to be kept by others, in their position of subordination
to him. But God had also communicated to them a knowledge of his secret purposes, which are called " mysteries."
This does not mean " things incomprehensible," but
" things undiscoverable by man, though capable of being
comprehended when revealed." Such a mystery is the
answer to the inquiry—What would become of the saints
alive upon earth at Christ's appearing ? None knew, till it

was revealed to Paul, who states it for our illumination · 1 Cor. xv, 51.

From this passage then we learn that ministers are not to be regarded as *priests*, mediating between God and man. They are not persons ordained, or men set apart to offer up prayer on behalf of "the laity," privileged, by virtue of their peculiar sanctity, to draw nearer to God than the common believer. Nor are they consecrated to "administer the sacraments." The Church of England does indeed speak of these "sacraments" as mysteries. "He hath instituted and ordained holy *mysteries*, as pledges of his love, and for a continual remembrance of his death, to our great and endless comfort." But this is unscriptural. The rites of Christ are never called "sacraments" in Scripture; much less "mysteries." Doctrines alone are called mysteries in Scripture. So far from apostles being sent to "administer the Sacraments," Paul tells us that he was not sent to baptize, but to preach the Gospel. He was sent to "make all know the economy of the mystery which was hid from ages," but then first fully disclosed: Eph. iii. In the full sense then, the passage before us supposes immediate communications of God's will. But Christ's ministers now know his will, and understand his mysteries, only by study of the Scriptures with prayer for the Spirit's aid.

For this office of stewardship the prime qualification is faithfulness. Scripture is as wise in what it omits to say, as in what it says. As the great preparation for the Christian ministry, it exacts, neither collegiate education, nor a genteel position in society, nor superior abilities, nor eloquence. Its demand is a spiritual one, "faithfulness."

Intellect in a steward is good, if combined with trustiness. Without it, the servant is only able the more completely to misuse the property entrusted to him. But one possessed of the feeblest understanding may deal honestly. As such he must be respected, even though he may judge but poorly what is best for his master's interests.

3. " But to me it is a very small thing that I should be judged*
by you, or by man's day,† yea, I judge not mine own self.   4.
For I am not conscious to myself of anything ; ‡ yet am I not
hereby justified ; but he that judgeth me, is the Lord."

Estimates may be formed of a minister's faithfulness by
four different parties.   These are now presented to us, and
the value to be attached to each is calculated for us.

The four estimates are these. 1. That of the world ; 2.
That of the church ; 3. A minister's own conscience ; 4.
The Lord.

1. The judgment of the world is, of course, the lightest
of all.   Paul speaks of it as a being examined by " man's
day."   A remarkable expression ! The present is " man's
day."   God is leaving him to himself ; to his own counsels,
and thoughts, and discoveries.   The builders of Babel are
permitted to lay their plans, to make their bricks, to collect
their bitumen, and to discover their enmity against God.
It is man's day, to prove to all what he is.   But soon this
day is to come to an end ; and to be replaced by " *the Day
of the Lord.*"   " The Lord alone shall be exalted in *that
day.*"   And it is to take effect upon all his contrivances,
and on all that he accounts great and glorious ; proving
to him, in spite of his unwillingness to receive the hateful
truth, that he cannot regenerate the world, or make himself
happy, or shield off God's judgments, or by wisdom find
out God.   The Lord is coming out of his place to see the
tower which men build, and not only to scatter as before,
but to smite and destroy Babel, and its builders.

The result of man's day will be, to increase his pride, his
stout-hearted unbelief, and independence of God.   But
that presumption will be checked, that pride be stained, by
" the great and terrible day of the Lord."   After man has
shown what he is, it is fitting that God should show what he

* Ανακρινω.   The word signifies to examine.

† Ημερας.

‡ Ουδεν γαρ εμαυτῳ συνοιδα.

is. And he will do it in judgment. Then, and not till then the nations of earth will learn righteousness. Rev. xv.

Now there is an estimate which man forms of his fellow. The world forms its judgment about the ministers of Christ. It discusses their merits, as learned, or talented, or faithful, or eloquent, or zealous, or bold, or hot-headed, just as it would treat any other topic of the day. Such judgment Paul regarded not. He cared neither for its applause or its censure. Its very standard of judgment was wrong; how then could it discern aright? The judgments of the present time are not to abide; they belong only to the fleeting period of " man's day."

2. But another estimate of a minister's faithfulness may be formed by *the church*. This is a far more correct opinion. Believers in Christ know something of the mind of God. To them it is given to know what God loves, what he hates, and the principles on which Christ will administer judgment at last. Their standard, as possessed in the Scripture, is perfect. .

But even this judgment was little esteemed by Paul. It was very shifting. Now the Galatians would have plucked out their eyes to give him. Yet a few years, and they sympathized with the apostle's enemies, gave way to false doctrine, and came near to abandoning the great centre truth of Christianity. But, even if the church's judgment were constant, it must fail of attaining to any great value on this point. It cannot read the heart. And a minister's faithfulness is a question of the heart. It can only guess at the character of the householder and the proceedings of the interior of the house, by what passes outside.

If the decision of the Lord had been merely a confirmation of the sentence of the church, then indeed the approval of its members would have been of the very highest importance. But, as it is, their most lofty opinion of a servant of his will not exalt him in Christ's eyes. Nor will their severest condemnation foreclose the question of his guilt. The whole matter will be tried on a new footing, in which their approval or rejection will find no place. It is possible he may have won the good opinion of his fellow-believers by conduct of much unfaithfulness. It is possible that he may have taken a course which he knew to be popular, while conscience condemned it, as disapproved of Christ. It is possible, that the heaviest odium may fall on a servant of Christ for principles and conduct which are wholesome, and profitable to the churches.

Paul therefore cared very little even for the church's estimate. It was a very little thing. It was but for a moment. It would not influence the judge's decision. It was only a *guess* at the apostle's motives, founded on more or less of evidence. He durst not be guided thereby. He must at times cross their thoughts, and rebuke their practices, drawing down on himself their momentary displeasure. They knew but few of the facts ; nothing of the seerets of his heart. Doubtless the history of his sufferings, as sketched in the close of the second Epistle, was quite new and startling. How unfit then were they to be judges !

3. But there was yet a higher tribunal. The conscience ! Is not that supreme ? No. " I judge not mine own self." You Corinthians have been debating about my faithfulness as God's steward. But you are not competent judges. As you read not the motives, this question is above your decision. Even my own decision is not final here. It is true I am conscious of my motives : I can call them before the bar of reflection. But even this estimate is not to be relied upon. It is not the sentence that is to stand. It is not the supreme court of appeal. Conscience has indeed authority to call each word, thought, action, in to its court, and to pass sentence thereon. The secret springs of action in each may by self-examination be known to each. This judge then is far more to be depended on than thousands of verdicts given from without. It is able to give us calmness

when assailed unjustly by those who know not the true state of the case.

But, superior as this tribunal is to the other two, Paul exposes its insufficiency. He could indeed rejoice in the testimony of a good conscience, that in simplicity and godly sincerity, he had lived before the churches. He could assert it as an example to the Ephesian elders. But he durst not trust it as a sure echo of the great sentence, to be passed by the Lord himself, at his appearing. He was "indeed unconscious to himself of any thing." No sense of duties left undone, or doctrines kept back through fear or self-interest, weighed down his spirits. From the first he had been obedient to the heavenly vision. From the opening of his commission he had successfully exercised himself in keeping his conscience always void of offence.

But though conscience did not accuse him of duties left undone, or of offences of a positive kind; though it bore record of zeal the most untiring, and of boldness that daily perilled life, yet this was not sufficient for acquittal before Christ. He was acquitted indeed, even by the verdict of impartial conscience. But there is a higher and final judge.

4. "He that judgeth me is the Lord." Jesus will adjust my place, not for life or death eternal, but in regard of my reward. His standard will be perfect. His knowledge embraces every thing. His sentence will be the unbiassed verdict of Truth and Righteousness.

5. "Therefore judge nothing before the time, until the Lord come, who both will bring to light the hidden things of darkness, and will make manifest the counsels of the hearts; and then shall each have (his) praise from God."

All judgment of motives is now out of season. It is "before the time." These shall indeed be one day settled. They are questions of the highest moment. But they belong to another dispensation, and other parties than the saints. God is not unmindful of his ministers' trustworthiness:

but now is the time of making proof of each. Hereafter shall be the decision concerning him. It shall be when the Lord comes. We are to be working ourselves, not passing sentence on the faithfulness of others.

Jesus alone is fit for this "high argument." There are two points necessary for the settlement of the faithful character of each, which are not possessed by the believer. He who would give a perfect decision must know—(1) The secret life of each. (2) The thoughts of the heart.

Some men and ministers are better in secret than they appear to others. The world and the church see only their consistent life, and powerful ministry. They know not their secret life of prayer and good works. The Saviour then, when he comes, will bring into open day the concealed portion of their life. "For there is nothing hid that shall not be known." And this manifestation of their hidden acts shall be for their glory. "Thy Father which seeth in secret, shall reward thee openly."

But there are other ministers whose best side is visible. They live for the eyes of their fellows, and the secrets of their life would bring them disgrace. To these, the broad light of heaven flung upon their unworthy deeds, will bring shame and woe.

2. But there is another attribute necessary to a perfect adjustment of the question. The motives of the heart must be known, ere the completeness of fidelity can be manifested. Jesus then will make manifest "the counsels of the heart." He will show the inner man and his purposes, as well as the actions, which men may have beheld. Many plans and efforts for good have been hindered and wrecked by untoward circumstances, and death. These will be recognized; and, where right, commended. There will be a scrutiny of *motives*. The counsels of the heart are God's peculiar province. They are the soul of every action. The body of the act may be seen by man, but its value for good or evil can only be perfectly calculated from within.

"Then shall each have (his) praise* from God." The rendering "every *man*" creates confusion. Alas, not every *man*, will be praised by God!

The context shows that believing ministers are meant. To all of those who have really been faithful, suited praise, exactly according to their due, shall be rendered. "Each" shall be dealt with. The motives and deeds of every minister shall be settled individually. To each, according to his heart and his work, shall recompense be rendered. Before, the judgment of *doctrine* was in question. Here we learn that *motives*, or fidelity, will be put to the test.

Solemn day! Some pastors, who enjoyed the full popularity of the world, and of the church of their day, will find that there is a wide difference between the sentence of Jesus, and the sentiments of men. Some faithful servants on the other hand, despised, misrepresented, maligned, will receive the approval of the great Investigator of the heart!

Solemn day! How momentous for the future are the thoughts of the heart; how abiding the consequences of our actions! Our post in the kingdom, will display, like an armorial bearing, to all beholders, what our place in the world has been. How should every rising of what the Saviour will disapprove, be checked and silenced by the thought of that day, which will bring to light every motive, and draw off the veil from every concealed act!

For the present, darkness hangs, and is intended to hang, its thick drapery of mist over half the life of every one. But the rising of the Sun of Righteousness shall scatter it. What will the consequence be to each, when the curtain is lifted?

Blessed is it, that the Lord Jesus shall decide the whole question! How, at times, the heart sighs amidst the misrepresentations of the prejudiced, for one that with full

---

* Olshausen says that επαινος means not praise, but recompense or requital generally. But he brings no proof of such a sense, either from the New Testament, or the classics.

knowledge and spotless impartiality, will adjudge the whole ! for one who knows the purity of our motives, when falsely coloured and maligned !

And what an assembly shall that be, before which this judgment shall be passed ! It shall make praise the sweeter and blame the sharper, that so many eyes of the nobles of heaven behold, so many ears are there to listen. How heavily shall every word of rebuke or even disapproval fall from the lips of the King of kings ! How joyous and glorious, the praise and the crown to the faithful pastor ? Is praise, even from our ignorant fellow-mortals, too potent a cup to be much drank of without intoxication ? What shall be the tingling of delight to hear it from the lips of Jesus, the crowned conqueror, in the presence of the Father and his angels !

CHAPTER VII

THE RACE AND THE CROWN

1 COR. IX, X.

IN the beginning of the ninth chapter of the first epistle to the Corinthians, Paul asserts his rights, as an apostle, to be maintained by the churches among which he laboured. "Not," he adds, "that I will press the right. On the contrary, none shall rob me of my boast, that I have preached to you, Corinthians, without charge. I act thus with an eye on the reward hereafter ; as well as that I may not hinder the progress of the Gospel now." In this spirit, though engaged in teaching and in pastoral visitation, he yet supported himself by working with his own hands, night and day.

Such a commencement of the chapter well introduces the subject of the close, wherein he incites believers in general, to conduct of like self-denial.

24. " Know ye not, that they who run in a race, all indeed run, but one (only) receiveth the prize ? So run, that ye may obtain."

The wisdom of God perpetually makes use of the things of time to shadow forth those of eternity. It is well known to all conversant with ancient history, that public games were celebrated in various parts of Greece, at which prizes were exhibited and contended for. The games consisted of leaping, running, wrestling, boxing, and the like. Of these, the Isthmian took place close to the city of Corinth.

To that sight multitudes from all parts of Greece were attracted, and both the candidates for the prizes, and the spectators, attached great importance to the reward. From this scene, perhaps then celebrating, the apostle draws instruction suited to *believers in general.*

"Know ye not?" As the Corinthians were proud of their knowledge, the apostle gently rebukes them by ten times asking them in this epistle—"Know ye not?" As though it were disgraceful for those who pretended to such intelligence, to be ignorant of the simpler truths which he enforces on them.

It is to be observed then, that there is a great and important resemblance between the Christian life and the Grecian games. Life, to the believer, rightly viewed, is to be a race. Christians are justified before God, as soon as they believe, independently of any good work; and their past evil deeds are blotted out by the blood of Jesus. But from the time of their being justified, they are set to please God, and to seek for an entrance into the coming kingdom of Messiah and reward in it. Their daily actions are telling upon that, either for good or for evil. The race of God's institution is open to all believers: not as in the games of Greece, to those only who could afford leisure and money; and whose frames were strong enough to give them a reasonable hope of success in the contest. Christians, be it observed, are to engage in the pursuit of God's reward, consciously and energetically. He is not running for the crown who does not know it, who is content just to be saved, and to move abreast of the low standard of Christian practice around him. The racers were not content to march on together in line.

But the apostle notices a remarkable difference between the games of men, and that appointed of God. The racers knew, that but one amidst their whole number could come off successful. If two or more reached the goal equal they must contend again, till one proved superior to the others. The rest must have spent their toil for nought. There was but one prize, and one victor. Hence each of them put forth his utmost energy. Every competitor must be overtaken and passed, or the superiority of fleetness over some was in vain.

This the apostle applies to us. It is not so in the race which God appoints. There not one only, but all that have run the race acceptably to the Most High, shall receive the crown. How great then the encouragement! Labour in the Lord shall not be in vain. Be therefore steadfast, and always abounding in his work!

But though all shall be crowned, who strive to the satisfaction of the Great Umpire of the games, yet let not this make you lax. Run as those racers do, who know that one only shall be rewarded. "So run"—with the same earnestness and perseverance. Or, the word may be connected with what follows—"Run *so* as to obtain." But I prefer the former view. "That *ye* may obtain;" for the prize is open to all. There are crowns in which all Christians will not share; for the New Testament mentions five kinds of crowns as the recompense for different kinds of service, or different exhibitions of Christian grace.

1. "THE CROWN OF GLORY" is proposed to those who, as elders or rulers of the churches, feed the flock of Christ, and oversee it: 1 Pet. v, 1-4.

2. "THE CROWN OF REJOICING" is to deck the head of those who have brought in souls to Christ: 1 Thess. ii, 19.

3. "THE CROWN OF RIGHTEOUSNESS" is proposed to all who have fought the good fight, kept the faith, and loved the appearing of the Lord Jesus: 2 Tim. iv, 7, 8.

4. "THE CROWN OF LIFE" is held out as the reward of all who endure temptation and martyrdom for Christ's sake: James i, 12; Rev. ii, 10.

But the crown before us—that of incorruption—is open to the striving of *all* believers. It is to be obtained by self-denial and victory over the lusts of the flesh.

25. " But every one that enters the lists* is temperate in all things. They indeed, that they may receive a corruptible crown, but we an incorruptible."

Instruction is made to flow to us, not only from the actual struggle for the prize, when the day of contest had arrived, but also from the training which preceded it. The object in submitting to the discipline, which was required of all the candidates, was to raise the powers of the body to their highest pitch. Now it was known by experience, that to produce this result, many things not naturally injurious to health must be abstained from. They must be temperate or self-denying. It was necessary to give up their liberty in a great degree. They were put under the control of an overseer of the combatants, who appointed for them their times of sleeping and rising, their meals, the quantity of their food, their times and places of exercise. By experience it was known what things were prejudicial to the vigour of the body, and these were to be carefully avoided. " They were temperate in *all* things."

Now the self-denial which they cheerfully exercised, the restraint under which they placed themselves in obedience to the master-passion—the desire of human glory—carry a lesson for us. In the hope of obtaining a corruptible crown, they trod under their feet, and kept subdued, the animal instincts of human nature. And shall not we for a far nobler crown, be content to deny our appetites ? to repress our pursuit and enjoyment even of things lawful, not that our bodies may be vigorous, but our souls prepared for glory ? Can the desire for human honour prompt to such sacrifices and exertions, and shall not the honour which cometh from God prove as strong a motive ? Temperance then and self-denial is to be a leading principle of the Christian life. But some Christians indulge in sleep, some in the pleasures of the table, some in the splendours of life, some in the more refined amusements of the world. Such

* Αγωνιζομενος.

are not racers for the crown. The self-indulgent are no candidates for this prize.

The comparative worthlessness, after all, of the prize which they sought, is next noticed by the apostle. Of what kind was the crown, which called forth such efforts? It was not of gold, nor even of silver; though Peter calls even these, our noblest metals, "corruptible things." It was a mere wreath of pine or wild olive, of laurel or parsley! But the crown for which we strive is one valuable in itself, never to fade.

26. "I therefore so run, not as uncertainly: so box I,* not as one that scourgeth† the air: 27. But I deal blows at my body, and lead it as a slave ;‡ lest by any means, after having acted the herald§ to others, I myself should become disapproved."‖

The apostle, having uttered his exhortations to his brethren, now discovers to us his own conduct, considered as himself a candidate for the prize in question.

He ran as vigorously, and with as sustained energy, as the Grecian racers. But he was not, as they were, under the depressing effects of uncertainty. They knew, as the condition of their contest, that while no exertion, self-denial, or endurance, might be wanting on their part, yet that an antagonist far less careful than themselves of the discipline of the training, might carry off the prize from them, by reason of his naturally more agile frame, or stouter lungs. Not so with Paul. He knew, that in the spiritual race before him, each candidate would be crowned who had acted in the spirit of the self-denial of the gospel.

In the next words he changes the figure. He is now no longer a racer, but a boxer. "So box I, not as one that scourgeth the air." He refers to those blows at an imaginary antagonist, which were delivered by way of practice in the training school; or those which just preceded the actual conflict. Or, perhaps the reference is, to those blows

---

* Πυκτευω. † Δερων. ‡ Υπωπιαζ . Δουλαγωγω.
§ Κηρυξας. ‖ Αδοκιμος γενωμαι.

which were aimed in the time of the fight, but which, being parried or misdirected, were struck in vain. But Paul did not, like the combatants of Greece, seek to bruise another's body, but to keep down his own.

"I deal blows upon my body, and lead it as a slave." The word used is a very graphic one, apparently one in use among the boxers. It signifies to aim blows at the face, and especially to give a black eye. Paul's blows, as the spiritual boxer, never missed : they were never given in ostentation. His fastings and watchings were not intended, as the fastings of the Pharisees, for ostentation. Did boxers plant their blows on the face, where they were most likely to tell ? So did Paul. He willingly put down all the glory of the flesh : inflicting suffering on his body in the cause of Christ by his ceaseless labours, fastings, watchings, endurance of cold and heat, and nakedness, stripes, and peril of life. He spared not his body, but sought to keep it in subjection. Lest his body should become his master, he made it his slave. The enslaving his body is still stronger, and marks the result of the former word. The contrary to this, he tells us, was the case with some. "For they are such as serve not our Lord Jesus Christ, but their own belly" : Rom. xvi, 18. "Mortify therefore your members which are upon the earth" Col. iii, 5.

But as hope cheered him on, so fear also joined its force in keeping him to his purpose.* Though all that run well shall be crowned, yet the Great Judge may esteem some unworthy of the crown : some, too, who once ran well. He feared then lest he should be found in this inglorious position. He felt, too, that in his case it would be still more grevious. He had occupied a very conspicuous position in the cause of Christ. He compares himself to the herald

---

* His "lest that by any means," of fear, answers to his "if by any means," of desire in Phil. iii. The object of hope is before him in the last, the object of fear in the present case. Both refer to the future kingdom.

of the games. The duties of that officer may be easily inferred from this passage—though hints concerning it are given in the classics. He would have to enrol and read aloud the names of the candidates, to place them at the starting point; to proclaim to them the conditions of the race, to give the signal for starting, and also to announce the name of the victor in each of the games. A similar position to this was filled by the apostle in the games proclaimed of God. Paul had invited many to the race · he had enrolled them for Christ, had taught them the conditions of the strife, had shown them the goal and the prize, had given them the signal to start, and exhortations to press on. How sad, then, if he were found at last unworthy of that prize to which he had cheered on so many!

He does not, in these words, tell us that he feared *the being cast into hell.* God's predestination of him as a believer, was his security against that. And in confidence of this, he flings down the gauntlet to the universe as unable to remove him from the love of Christ : Rom. viii. *There,* he was treating of the grace of God flowing forth from eternity. *Here,* he is discovering to us the influence of his own actions upon the future recompense of God, distributed on the principle of justice. It is not now the question of justification by faith to the ungodly ; but reward or loss in Messiah's kingdom to the saints. He might, though finally saved, yet be judged unworthy of a lot in the first resurrection. Or, though a place in that were granted, he might be accounted undeserving of a *crown.*

Here lies the mistake of most commentators. It is assumed, that there is no difference between reward and a bare salvation. It is taken for granted that " the crown " is only a figurative expression for simple salvation. It is supposed, that " eternal life " and the " kingdom of God " are the same thing. Thus Barnes, on this passage says, " The doctrine here taught is, the necessity of making an effort to secure *eternal life.* The apostle never thought of entering *heaven* by indolence or by inactivity. He urged bv every possible argument the necessity of making an exertion to secure *the rewards of the just*." (1) " The work of *salvation* is difficult." (2) " The danger of losing *the crown of glory* is great. Every moment exposes it to hazard, for at any moment we may die. (3) The danger is not only great, but it is *dreadful*. If any thing should arouse man, it should be the apprehension of *eternal damnation and everlasting wrath*."

On such assumptions, passages like the above present very great, or, we may say, *insuperable* difficulties to the Christian reader. Not that even insuperable difficulty is sufficient reason for our rejecting a doctrine made known by the testimony of God. But a view of the difference between eternal life and the kingdom of God disentangles the matter. The two portions of bliss are set on quite different grounds. Eternal life is the testimony chiefly to those *without*. The kingdom of Messiah in the dispensation of the fulness of times, is the prize offered to *the believer*.

Paul, as here ·addressing believers already the possessors of eternal life, is urging them on to the kingdom and its crown. His own desires were to attain both. For the crown is a reward distinct from the bare entrance to the kingdom. Some, I suppose, may enter millennial joys, yet not be crowned. Some Christian victors will have one crown ; some, perhaps, all the five.

The apostle's fear then, was not what is usually apprehended. " Paul," says Barnes, " had preached to thousands, and yet he felt, that after all this, there was a possibility that he might be *lost*." It is true, there was such a *possibility ;* but that is not what the apostle is now contemplating. The figure he makes use of will help to clear our views. The Isthmian race is over. One is victorious. A hundred have toiled along the course in vain. What now is to be done with these ? Are they to be scourged or imprisoned ? Are they to be sentenced to death ? By no means. No punishment whatever is theirs. They are rejected; (ἀδόκιμοι) esteemed unworthy of the prize they sought. *That is all.* It is loss enough, that they have expended so much time, ease, money, and strength in vain. Paul's fear then, was, lest he should be counted unworthy of the prize for which he lived. Possibly he might, by sin, be adjudged unworthy even to enter the kingdom. Or, we might imagine even a worse case of wilful transgression, such as that implied in the parables of the faithless steward, and the slanderous possessor of the one talent. Then there would be, as we learn from the Saviour's words, not only exclusion from the kingdom, but actual infliction of punishment during it.

Rejection or disapproval (ἀδόκιμος) is a relative term, which varies in its extent of meaning with the circumstances in relation to which the trial is made. In some cases it signifies the damnation of the parties rejected. Thus Paul speaks of some " reprobate *with reference to the faith* ": 2 Tim. iii, 8. Here, to be rejected, is to be lost. So again, where he speaks of some as " reprobate *with reference to every good work* ": Tit. i, 16. Here also, to be reprobate, is to be lost. But where the trial proposed was of a believer's fitness for office, there to be rejected did not involve eternal death : 1 Tim. iii, 10. Or again, with regard to a teacher's doctrine, if his foundation be good, the loss of his superstructure by fire shall not involve his own destruction : 1 Cor. iii. In the present instance, then, the trial proposed being only of Paul's fitness for the prize, the simple rejection, while entailing grief, would involve no infliction from God.*

But strange and sad it were for Paul, in the great day of Jesus' appearing, to see one after another of those whom he had led to the race called up to receive the victor's crown ; he himself meanwhile, the herald and instrument of their

---

* Ἀδόκιμος here stands opposed, not to election to eternal life, but to election to the crown, as worthy or unworthy.

joy, compelled by the Righteous Judge to stand aside, with drooped and dishonoured head!

This fear of the apostle's was no chimerical one. Actual fact sustained his solicitude. Who was the herald of the host of Israel? Who was sent of God to call them out of Egypt? Who marshalled them through the sea, and led them to meet with God at Sinai, their leader through the desert? But this same Moses was not permitted to obtain the prize. Though he besought with earnestness, he was refused. "Speak to me no more of this matter." He was rejected, though a herald to others.*

1. "For† I would not have you ignorant, brethren, that our fathers were all under the cloud, and all passed through the sea, 2. and were all baptized into Moses in the cloud and in the sea, 3. and all ate the same spiritual food, and all drank the same spiritual drink; (for they used to drink ‡ of the spiritual rock that followed them; but the rock was the Christ.")

It is evident from the drift of the epistle, that the Corinthians were going astray from too lax ideas of Christian liberty, and from an undue confidence in the power of human nature. From former passages we learn, that some attended idol feasts in the temples, and justified their so doing to the apostle. The tone of their hearts, as we gather from the tenor of the rebuke, seems to have been self-confident—"Trust us, Paul! Though we are present at the feasts in the idol's temple, yet we despise an idol as nothing. We see too clearly the absurdity of idolatry, we are too deeply pledged to Christ, by his gifts, by our baptism into his name, and our sitting at his table, ever to fall back into the gross superstition in which we were nurtured."

But their presumption was not shared by the apostle. Human power and will suffice for the earthly race, but

---

The rejection of Moses, it will be granted, does not suppose eternal destruction.

† Γαρ, is the reading of all the critical editions.

‡ Επιον, the first time; επινον, the second.

not for the divine. In order to abate it, he offers to their study the example of Israel, which they had overlooked or forgotten; but which God designed to be a standing witness of the weakness of the flesh, and of his condemnation of its evil ways.

The succeeding chapter is very closely connected with the preceding verses, by the critically accredited reading, " *For* I would not have you ignorant, brethren, that all our fathers were under the cloud." The apostle had stated his own apprehensions of a sad issue to himself, if he indulged in laxity of life. He was afraid of being disapproved at the close. He now sustains that apprehension, by the history of Israel in the desert.

As the forcibleness of every example consists in its being really like the case in hand, the Holy Spirit asserts the remarkable correspondence that exists between their position in the wilderness, and ours now.

We are now, what Israel was then, *the people of God*. We are now, as they were then, *redeemed by the blood of the Lamb*. They were brought out of Egypt, in order to pass through the wilderness to their promised rest in Canaan. We have left the world as our dwelling place, to regard it as the desert, through which as pilgrims, we are moving to our rest.

But, as the Corinthians seem to have thought much of the rites of Christ as pledging them to him, and securing them from ever departing from him, the apostle shows, that the tribes had some privileges, miraculously granted of God, corresponding with what we now enjoy. In speaking of the fathers as under the cloud, and baptized into Moses, both in the cloud and the sea, Paul seems intending to point out, that they had types, both of the birth of the Spirit, and of that of water. The cloud was the place of the Divine Presence. It *separated them from the Egyptians*, taking them under its powerful wings. The passing through the sea, too, was a type of the birth out of water.

But they had also something corresponding, in a measure, to the Lord's Supper. They had miraculous bread, the corn of heaven. They had also spiritual drink.

These things answer, moreover, to those Divine realities which are the spiritual sustenance of God's people now. Jesus is the true bread, that came down from heaven, on which his people now feed. The Holy Spirit answers to the miraculous water, whereby the thirsty thousands of the chosen people were supported. The rock was the figure of Christ. And, as from the stricken rock the water flowed, so it is from a pierced Messiah that the Holy Spirit proceeds to strengthen the people of God.

Thus they were as much pledged to Moses by the miraculous passage of the Red Sea, as we by the baptism into Christ. As that miracle by *one* stroke, never to be repeated, for ever cut them off from Egypt; they possessed a something typical of our one baptism. And as they had a *continuous* supply of bread and water suited to their need, so is that analogous to the Supper of the Lord with us.

The expression, "they drank of the spiritual rock *that followed them*," is singular. It probably refers primarily to the *water* from the rock. The rock whence the water flowed was situated in Rephidim, on high ground, at the foot of Sinai. From this it has been supposed, I think with justice, that the spot was chosen, with a view to its general elevation, and suitability of position, in order to afford Israel a constant supply, as they descended to the lower levels of the wilderness.

But the "spiritual rock," which the material rock prefigured, was Messiah. The rock of nature abode in its place. But the Lord journeyed with them in the pillar of the cloud, to bring them on their way.*

---

* Here we have a good answer to the usual argument of the Roman Catholics drawn from those words—" This is my body." " The rock was Christ." Do they believe that the rock was transubstantiated into Christ?

5. " But with the majority* of them God was not well pleased ; for their (bodies) were strewn in the wilderness."

The Holy Spirit has exhibited, in brief but forcible words, the great and miraculous deliverance experienced by God's people of old ; and the pledges under which God laid them, to obey Moses as their leader. If any people might have presumed, from God's mercies to them, that they should never fall, and that God would never smite them, however they might offend him ; Israel was that people. But the privileges bestowed on them did not set them above the demands of the Divine equity. Something was expected from them in answer to the grace displayed on their behalf. Gratitude, obedience, and the desire to please Jehovah, might justly be looked for as the requital for his mercies.

But these righteous expectations were disappointed. Rebellion marks their progress through the desert. " With the majority of them," therefore, " God was not well pleased." The wilderness put them on their trial. " The Lord thy God led thee these forty years in the wilderness to humble thee and *to prove thee, to know what was in thine heart*, whether thou wouldst keep his commandments, or no " : Deut. viii, 2. The race is the trial of a man's speed. The judge's decision is manifested at the issue.

The five times repeated " all "—" *all* our† fathers were under the cloud ; *all* passed through the sea ; *all* were baptized into Moses ; *all* did eat the same food ; *all* drank the same drink ; " seems intended to carry back our minds to the verse with which this exposition began. " They which run in a race run *all*." We are invited to behold, under what very favourable circumstances God started his people on their race. But the issue is sad. It is almost like that of the Grecian games. " But *one* receiveth the

---

* Τοις πλειοσιν.

† Why, " *our* fathers " when they were Jews, and Paul was writing to Corinthians ? Is it because the apostle is speaking as a Jew ?

prize." No like necessity of condition existed in their case ; but the result was, that but two, out of perhaps two millions, entered the land of promise. Marvel not then, if it should appear, that this doctrine carried into execution will cut off many Christians from the reward.

The assertion, that God was not well pleased with the main body of Israel, is equivalent to saying that they were rejected.* God was the Great Umpire of the race to which he called them, and he accounted them unworthy of the prize.†

His displeasure was exhibited in act. Their carcases strewed the wilderness, though the prospect of entering the land was held forth as the hope that beckoned them on. But his rejection of them was not a piece of simple sovereignty. It was deserved by them. And the grounds of his rejection are then stated. As five special mercies of God to Israel have been named, so five special executions of wrath on the castaways are exhibited by the apostle.

6. " Now these things took place‡ (as) our examples, that we should not lust after evil things, as they too lusted."

Israel stumbled and fell. God reckoned their fall as no light matter. He wrote his indignation in the broad characters of miraculous judgments. As we have seen the mercy that started them on their race, so is it shown also, that want of temperance was their ruin " *They lusted after evil things.*" God gave them good gifts. But they desired the meat of Egypt, which they had left. " They desired flesh for their lust." The Lord cut them off by a plague, while yet the meat was in their mouths : Numb. xi. The

* The αδοκιμος of ix, 27, corresponds to the ευδοκησεν of this verse.

† Herein they were the opposite of Jesus, over whose head, in the hour of Transfiguration the Father pronounced these words :—" This is my beloved Son, *in whom I am well pleased.*" ευδοκησα : Matt. xvii, 5. 2 Pet. i, 17.

‡ Εγενηθησαν.

place was called thenceforward by the melancholy name of Kibroth Hataavah, " THE GRAVES OF LUST ! "

In the last verses of the former chapter the apostle had set forth natural intelligence as demanding temperance of those who sought to be crowned. But now he manifests the same conclusion by the inspired history of Israel, who, owing to the want of this self-denial, were rejected from the crown.

These things were meant as lessons to us. Their position of mercy is typical of ours. It is intended to affect our judgments and our hearts. It is designed to reflect our standing and condition as in a mirror ; that the natural deceptiveness of the heart, which abides, in measure, even with the regenerate, should not parry the strong appeal thence derived. It furnishes a lasting proof of God's *determination to deal, even with his redeemed people, on the footing of their works, in regard to the prize held out to them.*

See enforced hereby the lesson which Paul carried out so practically in his own case. Many of the chosen people fell in the wilderness, under the displeasure of the Lord, because they lusted after evil things. Paul, therefore, fearful of thus provoking the Most High, not only did not seek after *evil* things, but curbed and denied himself, even in regard to things *lawful.* Not only he did not make himself dissatisfied by craving something worldly not yet bestowed ; he withdrew within the circle of things already granted, and exercised self-denial there. Had Israel so acted, never had they so fallen.*

In all the instances mentioned here God cut off the offenders *by death ;* entirely removing thus their hopes of entering the land of promise. Hence we are to understand the cases cited as applying to us in the strongest sense :

---

* In the present passage we have the Holy Spirit's enforcement of *temperance ;* but abstinence from alcohol, in which so many now make it mainly to consist, is not so much as named.

that is, that those believers who are guilty of like trespass, will forfeit altogether their entrance into the kingdom.

It is not to be supposed that the sins specially mentioned here, however, are *all* the sins that will exclude from the thousand years. Those acts of transgression in Israel's history are adverted to which most bore upon the then existent transgressions of the Corinthian church. Many others might be mentioned as, for example, the rebellion of Korah, Dathan, and Abiram, against Moses and Aaron. In that also the issue was supernaturally fatal.

Let us then in our day beware of lusting after evil things. Let us not seek the world's fame, pleasures, or gold. We have left Egypt; let us not remember again its flesh-pots with desire. *There* dwelt bondage and death; before us lie life and glory.

7. " Neither become ye* idolaters, as did some of them ; as it is written, ' The people sat down to eat and to drink, and rose up to play.' "

The scene referred to is that of the festival before the molten calf at the foot of Sinai : Ex. xxxii. There Israel, although in the presence of that very mount from whose top God had, with voice of thunder, forbidden any representation of himself, made the calf of gold. Their sitting down and their rising up were both for sin. By their beginning to play, after the feasting was over, we are to understand their dancing. So it is afterwards explained. When Moses came down from the mount, it is said, " As soon as he came nigh unto the camp, he saw the calf and the *dancing* ": v. 19.

It seems probable, from the quotation subjoined, that the apostle especially intended to touch the conscience of the lax Corinthians, who were present at the idol-feasts. The chapter of Exodus which we are considering, is a standard whereby to discover what idolatry is. But in this

* Γίνεσθε.

description of what provoked God and Moses, we are not informed directly of their bowing before the calf, or kissing it. We read only of feasting in its presence, and then dancing in honour of it. Now, while the latitudinarian Corinthian believers doubtless kept themselves from all direct worship of the god or goddess into whose temple they entered, yet they ate and drank there. But having done so much, they were doubtless expected by their heathen friends to go a step further. "They could not be so un-neighbourly and unpolite as to refuse to join in a harmless dance after their meal was over." But if they complied, they had then completed that very picture of the offence of which Israel was guilty—that offence, which broke the covenant, and drew down the wrath of God. They were guilty of a sin, which called forth the sword of Levi, and cut off three thousand. Thus wonderful is the reach of the word of God. That scripture, though written so long before, described and denounced as hateful idolatry, a practice which the careless saints of Corinth thought so harmless.

From this passage I gather a confirmation of the view given with regard to the prize of which the apostle speaks. I have supposed it to signify the future kingdom of glory. Now in another portion of this epistle we are taught that some of the sins above specified will shut us out of the *kingdom*. "Know ye not that the unrighteous shall not inherit *the kingdom of God?* Be not deceived: neither *fornicators*, nor *idolaters*, nor adulterers, nor effeminate, nor abusers of themselves with mankind, nor thieves, nor covetous, nor drunkards, nor revilers, nor extortioners, shall inherit *the kingdom of God* ": 1 Cor. vi, 9, 10.

8. " Neither let us commit fornication, as some of them committed ; and fell in one day three and twenty thousand."

The reference in this place is to the history of Israel's intercourse with the daughters of Moab, after the desire of

Balaam and Balak to curse Israel had been baffled : Numb. xxv, 1-9. In the present warning of the Holy Ghost, idolatry and fornication stand closely connected. So were they in the history of Israel. "The people began to commit whoredom with the daughters of Moab. And they called the people to the sacrifice of their gods : and the people did eat and bowed down to their gods." These two sins are also connected in the way of God's judgments. Those who degrade his glory by idolatry, are given up to vile affections : Rom. i, 25, 26.

The anger of the Lord was, in consequence, greatly kindled, and he commanded the ringleaders' heads to be cut off ; while he himself sent a plague on the dissolute libertines of his people. "There fell in one day twenty-three thousand."*

The sin of fornication was one to which the city of Corinth was peculiarly addicted ; against which, therefore, the more urgent warnings were required. Several passages discover to us, that this sin will greatly prevail in the latter days. It will be defended and extended by the aid of false doctrine, and into it some of the people of God will fall. Let us not then be deceived with vain words ; but read God's anger against it, expressed in his judgment on Israel because of it. Note the extremity of his wrath in the suddenness of the stroke. The offenders fell "*in one day.*" The murmurers and tempters of God were spared for some time ; but these were struck down at once.

9. " Neither let us tempt the Christ,† as certain also of them tempted, and were destroyed by the serpents."†

---

* A difference of a thousand is found between the two numbers as stated by the apostle and by Moses : Numb. xxv, 9. This may be accounted for by the slain being an intermediate number, between 23,000 and 24,000. But I prefer to suppose with some that 23,000 fell *in one day*, the other thousand being cut off on the next day, or on some of the following ones.

† The article occurs both before " Christ " and " serpents."

Many times did the redeemed people tempt the Lord. But the temptation which was avenged by the well-known fiery serpents, took place towards the close of their sojourn in the desert. Numb. xxi, 4. Their bite was mortal. Much people of Israel died. The remedy appointed for this sin was the type of the future good news to a dying world. John iii, 14, 15.

But what is meant by tempting God ? It signifies the trying experiments with him—the putting him into positions of difficulty, to compel him to display his powers or his character. It may arise either from unbelief or presumption. Thus a servant is tempted, when a master throws money unguarded in his way, to try if he is honest. Israel tempted Jehovah, when they thought they could ask something of him beyond his power to perform. Achan tempted him when he thought that the eye of Jehovah could not detect his theft. Similar was the sin of Ananias and Sapphira, in later times.

This warning against tempting Christ applied especially to the Corinthians, who entered as guests into the temple of false gods, after dedicating themselves to the true God and his Son.

God is tempted now, when his people throw themselves into scenes of temptation to which duty calls them not ; because they believe themselves elect, and therefore secure finally, however they may fall by the way. But the present view enables us to perceive how God can punish even those whom he finally receives to eternal life. THERE ARE A THOUSAND YEARS IN WHICH GOD MAY RECOMPENSE TO HIS SAINTS THE DEEDS DONE IN THE BODY.

From this passage it appears probable, that believers who marry an unbeliever will be excluded from the reign of Messiah, as being tempters of Christ.

10. " Neither murmur ye, as certain also of them murmured, and were destroyed by the destroyer."

The people murmured often. At Marah, because the

waters were bitter ; at Sin, because they wanted food ; at Rephidim, because there was no water ; at Kadesh, in the rebellion of Korah. But the chief murmuring, which drew down on them the oath of exclusion, was that which occurred on the return of the spies. The Lord bid the tribes go up, and take possession of the land. But they refused. They alleged that God only meant to destroy them, by setting them to face difficulties so insuperable. This was the last drop in their cup of iniquity. The Lord, in his anger, sware that they should not go up, but their carcases should fall in the wilderness. This example of Israel's sin, and of the displeasure of the Lord, appropriately comes the last. That, and the oath of indignation which it drew from Jehovah, is the especial theme of warning in Heb. iii, iv.

Who is " the Destroyer," by whom the rebels were cut off ? Whether it be a good or an evil angel, does not appear. But the being who cut off the Egyptian first-born, when those of Israel were spared, is called by this name. " For the Lord will pass through to smite the Egyptians ; and when he seeth the blood upon the lintel, and on the two side posts, the Lord will pass over the door, and will not suffer *the Destroyer* to come in unto your houses to smite you " : Ex. xii, 21. His own people then, for their offence, are at length treated as Egyptians.

Various sins seduced different parties of the offenders ; and different punishments, but all with the same fatal issue, awaited them. Let us chiefly beware of the sin that most easily besets us !

11. " Now all these things happened unto them as examples ; but they were written for our admonition, unto whom the ends of the ages have arrived.* 12. Wherefore, let him that thinketh he standeth take heed lest he fall."

1. These things happened as examples of warning to *the remnant of Israel.* The offenders themselves were cut off :

* Εις ους τα τελῆ των αιωνων κατηντησεν.

no amendment was intended for *them*. But these divine judgments were designed to make Israel fearful of provoking the holy God that dwelt in their midst. That lesson they were slow to learn.

2. They happened also as examples to us, and examples in two especial points of view.

i. They show *the tendencies of the redeemed to sin*. When we read the history of Israel, we are ready to flatter ourselves, that so sensual, besotted, and rebellious a people, is not to be found elsewhere on the globe. But He who looks at the heart, beholds all their perverseness mirrored afresh, in the history of the church of Christ. Lest we should grow proud in vain thoughts of ourselves, He has taught us that these sins of old have their types still among his people now. Let us then, as individuals not be high-minded, but fear. Our tendencies to evil are the same as theirs.

ii. But these things were written chiefly, to manifest *the character of our God*. To Israel he displayed abundant mercy, and avouched them to be his people before the heathens around. But his mercy did not shut out the exercise of equity. A father's love does not destroy the rod. He may even disinherit the presumptuous. The strong hand-writing of facts compels us to see, that there is a limit to the forebearance of God towards his own chosen ones. After the people have ten times provoked him, the door is closed beyond the hope of its re-opening. This is the counterpart to that contrary process which is going on in regard to the obedient. God's eye is on his servant Abraham after he has first believed, noting his several acts of submission and subjection to his will from time to time. He expresses, by words of encouragement, his good pleasure ; till at length, the last act of compliance being fully rendered, he, with oath never to be forgotten or set aside, gives to Abraham the promise of the kingdom of Messiah : Gen. xxii.

Let us then well understand, that privileges are not intended to lull us to sleep ; that the blessed reality of the election of God will prove no security to elect offenders.

See here also an answer to a subtle encouragement which unbelief derives from the multitude of the offenders. We are always ready to comfort ourselves with the numbers that hold an opinion, or unite in a practice. Either we shall be overlooked amidst the many, or the stroke will not descend, when a crowd of criminals must be stricken. The idea is often realized in the transactions of human governments. Numbers may overawe a human monarchy, or compel it to express its displeasure by vengeance executed only on the more prominent of the criminals. But not so with God. His omnipotence regards not, whether the rebellious body be a host, a world, or an individual.

As then the character of our God abides the same from age to age, we may see in his former procedure towards his people of the old covenant, how he will conduct himself towards his people of the new covenant, if their demeanour resemble that of the tribes in the desert.

" Give me FACTS," says the philosopher, when he wishes to understand the nature of anything. Facts must overturn all theories that stand opposed to them.

Here then is the character of our God, mapped out for us by the conspicuous land-marks of ancient and authentic facts. God himself has chosen them ; so that they are not exceptive examples, but *specimen facts,* designed to give us an insight into the judgments of the Most High. As he acted then, so will he act again under like circumstances. As long as the various forms of sin shall retain their nature, so long must they come into collision with the same perfection of the Divine Nature. God, as " the righteous judge," having marked out these sins of Israel as deviations from the racer's course, which excluded the guilty from the prize in former days, must hold to his decision still. If sin, with the imperfect light possessed by Israel was still so sinful ;

how much more, when committed by his people now against the stronger radiance of the Gospel!

While then we are reading the chronicles of Israel in the wilderness, we are like an inexperienced crew sailing with unerring pilot along a rocky, dangerous channel. "See you," he says, "those breakers? There one stormy night in December last struck the *East Indiaman*, and every soul was lost. A pistol-shot from the spot we this moment occupy lie sunken rocks. You see that buoy? It tells you where the *Juno* struck and went down, with every soul on board. To your left is a quick-sand, that has swallowed in times past and in my day, more ships than I can number." Counsels administered on the basis of such peremptory facts must command attention. Long as the sunken rocks shall lie there, so long must he who would carry his vessel safely into port, avoid them.

But this is not all. It is true, that these perfect dealings of God with his ransomed ones were expressed in the unmistakable language of facts. But thousands of facts of deep import, specially those of centuries long gone by, have perished. They are to us, as though they had never been. But God esteemed so highly the deep momentousness of these actions of his towards the tribes, that he commanded them to be recorded for us. He caused them to be written too by his Spirit, that no mixture of error, no omission of important features, no introduction of non-essential lines or colours, should mar the speaking picture. Ponder it, Christian! "It was written for our admonition." We too are men, girt in with privileges, our behaviour inspected ever by a Holy God, who expects us to render him again according to the benefit done unto us.

We have come to the last of the ages. The wisdom to be gathered from the preceding ones has been, by God's direction, garnered for us. If *they* were inexcusable, whose offences provoked God at the stations of the desert, how much more ours, if we offend in like sort! We pity the man who was first killed by the bursting of a steam boiler He knew not the gigantic strength of the power with which he was coping. But human wisdom recorded and treasured the fact, that steam compressed might not be trifled with. It sought to trace its laws, so as to escape danger from it; and it has succeeded. This point of human intelligence has its counterpart in the divine. Mighty are many of the creatures of God; destructive if used amiss, but healthful and full of utility, if made use of according to the laws ordained of God. How much more is the God with whom we have to do, mighty and worthy of all reverence and godly awe! If we understand aright his character, and abstain from those things which justly offend him, all his divine perfections are on our side. But if we transgress, the wrecks of former ages may assure us, that he will vindicate his own glory on us, as he did on the guilty ones of old.

This history of Israel, dictated by the Spirit of God, is a living thing. It has a voice for our day, as truly as for the survivors of the cloud-led camp. The echoes of the desert are ringing still. The inscriptions on the tombs of the cast-aways of the wilderness are legible to this day, graven by the finger of the Most High. And while the lore of Egypt may interest the learned, and the uncovered and decyphering monuments of ancient Assyria may amaze and delight, the memorials of the ransomed from Egypt are a better study. They teach us God. They show us that entrance into the kingdom of God is not for the careless and secure. Glorious is the prize proposed. But be not vain-gloriously confident. " Look at the precipices over which thousands have slipped and been lost: see the pits into which multitudes have fallen, and beware! The way is difficult—Lean not to your own powers!" "Let him that standeth take heed lest he fall." He has not yet got beyond the snares of his wily foe.

There is a testing now of God's people in the world's

wilderness, as of yore in that of Sinai. Let us walk humbly, prayerfully! Each event that befals us is a trial of our character and state. God's eye is upon us to see and to note how we meet them. No circumstances can arise so trying and perplexing, that we may not act rightly, and receive praise. Nor again, can any circumstances happen, in which we may not disgrace our profession, and draw down on our head, dishonour and rebuke in the presence of the Lord.

But I would end this chapter with a word of encouragement.

Could the uncertain prospect of glory from man and its coronet of fading leaves, animate the ancient racers and wrestlers to much certain self-denial, and incite them to contend with energy and constancy for so poor a prize? How much more should the certain assurance of glory from God, and his unfading crown, lead us to equal vigour and self-denial? That was a lofty hour in the life of the Grecian champion, when, with sounding trumpet, a herald preceded him, and proclaimed his victorious name! and when from rank to rank of the admiring spectators murmurs and shouts of applause broke forth, eyes glistened, hands greeted him, and flowers and wreaths were showered upon his head. But what is *that* to the grand assembly of angels and the risen righteous with Christ their triumphant Head, when the conquerors of the cross, despised now or unknown by man, then fresh in the brightness of immortality, draw near to receive their crowns of conquest from the hand of the King of kings and Lord of lords!

CHAPTER VIII

THE TENT AND THE HOUSE

2 Cor. v.

In the fourth chapter of the 2nd Corinthians, the apostle asserts his honesty in preaching the gospel. No sinister motive impelled him. He adhered to the ministry given him by God, in spite of many difficulties, perils, hardships. He persevered against all obstacles, in the hope of resurrection. He fainted not, though his strength failed under the united pressure of exertions and afflictions. But his soul partook not of the infirmities of the body. It grew in grace, in strength of hope and confidence continually. His present afflictions he counted light, in comparison with the weight of glory to come. Of course this is spoken of believers only. Endurance of trouble is no opening to glory for the unconverted and rebellious against God.

When pressed down by things visible, he looked at the things unseen. For the things of sense are passing away; but the things of faith shall abide. It is well to observe, that the " things which are not seen," do not mean things invisible, or incapable of being seen. For the new world and its new Jerusalem will one day be objects of sight. The apostle is contrasting only things which are now capable of being seen with things which cannot now be beheld, but must be received on the ground of faith.

2 Cor. v, 1. "For we know that if our earthly house of the tent* be dissolved, we have a building from God, a house not made with hands, eternal in the heavens."

Affliction might end in the apostle's being compelled to give up life itself for Christ. Under such circumstances, here is Paul's comfort. "If the present body be dissolved in death, a better body and an eternal one is ours." This is the general force of the sentiment. Of course this applies equally to the natural death of the believer at all times.

But let us consider the peculiarities of the verse. Our present body is called "the house of the tent." A tent is but a piece of canvas or cloth stretched upon one or more poles, and secured to the ground by pegs, as a temporary covering for those who would else sleep in the open air. It is a habitation without a foundation, soon moved by the owner, easily blown down, or torn up; in every way frail and insufficient.

Such is our present body. The soul is the man. The body is the tent under which the owner dwells. The destruction of the house is not the destruction of the inhabitant. It is a garment, which may be changed without prejudice to the wearer. This is the other figure which the apostle employs to discover to us the relation subsisting between the soul and the body. Death is the collapse of the tent, the breaking of its pole, the rent canvas lying in a useless heap. But the inhabitant survives. Driven out of an abode no longer suitable for him, he is to be introduced into another far more glorious.

"If it should be taken down we have another." Death is thought by the ungodly almost the only certain thing amidst a world of uncertainties. But to the believer there is one thing yet more sure. It is the coming of the Lord, at which his watchful people then alive will be suddenly changed, without passing through death. It is to this certainty, I suppose, that the apostle alludes, when he

* Οικια του σκηνους. There is no "this" in the original.

speaks of death as only possible or hypothetical. Not death, but the Lord's appearing, is to be the object before the believer's eye.

The future body is called, " a building from God an house not made with hands, eternal in the heavens." A house is far superior to a tent. Resting on a settled foundation, and composed of far less perishable materials, it may resist the force of the weather for centuries. But even that is not eternal. As made with men's hands, it partakes of the frailty of its maker, and lies in ruins at last. But the body which we are hereafter to wear, as it is a house not made with hands, so is it to be eternal.*

The present body is one of the seen things, and therefore only temporary. The future is reserved for us in heaven, and as being one of the things unseen, is eternal. The present body is suited to our earthly and animal life, but the body to come is to be adjusted to our spiritual and endless life.

The whole of this passage is important, as proving that not death, but the eternal body is to be the object of the believer's desire. The dissolution of this tent-like frame is not man's final farewell to a body. On the contrary, it is God's decree, permanently to fix him to one ! That day is to be the consummation of his happiness. God's own glory is bound up in this counsel of his. It must be proved, that evil belongs, not to the material creation, for which the Creator alone is responsible ; but to the spiritual and moral part of it.

2. " For in this we groan, earnestly desiring to be clothed upon with our house which is from heaven."

The two figures of a house and of a garment are combined in the verse before us. Perhaps the reason of this is, that

---

* Both tent and house are made by hands. Both our mortal and immortal bodies come from God. The relative superiority of one of the habitations constructed by man is made to illustrate the superiority of the future body to the present.

to have said "clothed with our garment," might have interfered with a passage which follows.

It needs no proof, that men in their present bodies groan. Believers, too, groan, not only from the pains to which our present bodies are exposed, but also at times through the inflictions of the persecutor.

But this groaning leads to the desire of the future body. The hope of the Christian is not the philosopher's desire to be delivered from the body, as the great impediment to intelligence, purity, and happiness. No: herein the Christian revelation occupies a position of antagonism to the vain theories of men. To be naked spirits is not the height of human felicity. It is when risen, body and soul united, that the consummation of life is to be attained.

In the former Epistle to the Corinthians, Paul had set himself to expose the false views entertained by some of the saints of that church, concerning the resurrection. Some of them, most probably through the misleading influence of Greek philosophy, denied the literality of the resurrection; and supposed it to mean the spiritual rising of the soul to newness of life, or the Swedenborgian notion, that the soul at death takes a spiritual body. Against that the apostle shows, that our future body is to be material, and that the change to the glorious body of resurrection is to take place at the same moment for both the living saints and the dead. *Here,* the subject is contemplated from another point of view; and while the spirit-state is admitted, it is yet declared not to be the ultimate hope of the Christian.

In the first Epistle, the intermediate state of the dead in Christ was passed over. Some then might have thought that Paul did not hold the doctrine; or a question might have been raised thereupon, what were his views respecting it? That silence of the former epistle then is here supplied. The spirit-state of the dead in Christ, though inferior to the resurrection-state, is yet an advance upon the present.

From the expressions made use of by the apostle, it

would appear, as if the future body of the believer were already in existence on high. " *We have* a building from God, an house not made with hands, eternal *in the heavens.*" " Earnestly desiring to be *clothed upon with our house which is from heaven.*" A succeeding verse seems to confirm the same view. The reader will consider whether the words used imply this. The comparison of the resurrection with the growth of a plant from a seed, though it give a wholly different view, must not be regarded as *contradictory* to any thing said here. No two words of God can really contradict one another ; for contradictions cannot both be true.

3. " If, at least, even when clothed, we shall not be found naked."

The time of being thus clothed from on high is at the descent of Christ from heaven, whence the living and the sleeping saints are to be gathered to him : 1 Thess. iv.

But if thus clothed with the celestial body, what room is there left for nakedness ? The clothing and the nakedness of the text are of different kinds. The clothing of the soul, then to take place, is a *physical* or *material* clothing, to be effected by God himself.

But immediately on our assuming the immortal body the Saviour will enter upon an inquiry as to our deeds. This is asserted still more broadly in the succeeding context.

It is assumed, then, that believers may be *spiritually* naked before Christ in the day of his appearing. Against this conclusion, I can see no just ground of objection. For it is certain, that Paul is treating of believers, and of them only, in the preceding and following context.

" *We* having the same spirit of *faith* " : iv, 13.

" All things are for *your* sakes " : 15.

" The inward man is renewed day by day " : 16.

" *We* look not at the things which are seen " · 18.

" *We* have a building of God " : v. 1 ; and so on.

But the contrary to this is generally assumed. It is

supposed impossible. " If nakedness refer to the spiritual state of the soul, or to its deeds in the body, the *wicked* alone must be meant." But our assumptions must not contradict the plain meaning of the word of God.

It is indeed true, that the righteousness of Christ imputed to the believer is a perfect answer to the demands of the law. On this footing, and when the question is concerning eternal life or eternal death, the apostle's challenge holds good—" Who shall lay any thing to the charge of God's elect ? It is God that justifieth. Who is he that condemneth ? "

But the trial of the believer before Christ at his appearing is not a trial for life or death. He is called up to give account of his life since he began to believe. He became virtually or by open profession a servant of Christ as soon as he believed. He makes answer to Christ himself. If, therefore, the Saviour demand of him—" How have you conducted yourself since you were my servant ? " It would be of no avail to reply—" Lord, thy righteousness is my plea." " I know it," might be the answer : " but I am inquiring what you have done since you took my righteousness as your defence against the just deserts of your sinful life." It is evident then, that the imputed righteousness of the Lord Jesus is no bar to the inquiry of the Lord Jesus into the conduct of those who shelter themselves beneath it. Presumptuous sins have been committed by not a few, resting upon the very security afforded by God's own plea. Have there not been Antinomian believers, who have sinned, because they were confident in the satisfaction made for sin ? Shall such high-handed trespassing go unpunished ? Jesus supposes his servants to be dealt with in the day of his judgment, not on the footing of God's provision made for their salvation ; but on their own deeds. What say the parables of the Talents, of the Steward, and of the Servants left waiting for their master ? Matt. xxiv, xxv ; Luke xii ; Mark xiii.

That *saints* may be found naked is proved by the word

of God "Thou knowest not," says Jesus in his Epistle to the church of Laodicea, "that thou art wretched, and miserable, and poor, and blind, and *naked*": Rev. iii, 17. And again, "Behold I come as a thief. Blessed is he that watcheth and keepeth his garments, *lest he walk naked,* and they see his shame": Rev. xvi, 15.

The expression, "we should be *found* naked," imports that solemn inquiry into the life of each believer, which is to take place before our Lord. The question will be sifted, and as the evidence shall appear, so will the cause be decided. The "finding," then, is a judicial term. So Abraham speaks concerning the Lord's visitation of Sodom —"Peradventure there shall be forty (righteous) *found* there?" "And he said, I will not do it, if I *find* thirty there" · Gen. xviii, 29, 30. So with regard to Joseph's cup. "With whomsoever of thy servants it is *found,* both let him die, and we will be my lord's bondmen." "The cup was *found* in Benjamin's sack": Gen. xliv, 9, 12.

It denotes also the responsibility of the saints, and that the question will be greatly as to his state of mind at the time of the investigation before the judgment-seat of Christ. Thus we have an explanation both of the certainty of the one clothing, and of the uncertainty of the other. The material clothing is from God, and is certain. But while the time of this change for eternity ought to be to every believer a time of joy, it will not be necessarily so to all, because the party is a believer. The era of the reconstruction of our body would be that of full bliss, if misconduct on our part since the day of our believing prevent not. Here then comes in the apostle's note of caution. There will be some spiritually unclothed before Christ. There will be some "ashamed before him" at his coming. To such unclothed ones, the day will be one of sorrow: while to others there will be an eternal weight of glory. These are recognized again afterward, as those "well-pleasing" to Christ. Certainty is secured, where we have the promise of God : uncertainty comes in where our works enter into the question.

4. " For we who are in the tent groan being burdened ; where-upon* we wish not to be unclothed, but to be clothed upon, that mortality might be swallowed up by life."

The dwellers in the present body groan. It is the time of burden and suffering. Nature, sin, and persecution combine oftentimes their trouble. Yet the troubles of life do not make us as believers covet death. Death is an unclothing. It is the putting off of a garment long worn, as we undress in going to sleep. But death in itself is not desirable, but rather dreadful to nature. Nor is it made the object of the believer's hope. The true object of desire is the eternal garment to be brought at the Saviour's descent from heaven. The new body is compared to another dress drawn over the old from above. But the issue is, not two simultaneously-existing bodies : but that the old is absorbed and effaced by the new. This is to take place, the apostle tells us, " in a moment, in the twinkling of an eye, at the last trump." Then " death is *swallowed up* in victory." The " swallowing up in victory " there, answers to the " swallowing up by life " here. The primary desire of the Christian then is, if the Lord be so pleased, that without tasting of death, he may suddenly be caught up to himself to meet him in air ; in an instant exchanging mortality and the scenes of earth, for the glory of the presence of Jesus. This would suppose the escape of death, or the separation of body and soul. " We who are in the tent," answers to the " we who are alive and remain," of 1 Thess. iv. There are those who are unclothed, or amongst the dead in Christ.

The apostle is discussing now only the case of those alive on earth at the Lord's return, which is one of the questions which engage him in 1 Cor. xv. But there he speaks also

* Eφ'ῳ. Our translators have transposed the words to get their sense.

and chiefly of the restoration of the dead. Hence he uses continually two expressions there to the one expression here. " This *corruptible* must put on incorruption, and this *mortal* must put on immortality. So when this *corruptible* shall have put on incorruption, and this *mortal* shall have put on immortality, then shall be brought to pass the saying that is written, Death is swallowed up in victory."

But here mortality alone is named, as describing the state of the saints exposed to death.*

4. " Now he who wrought us for this very thing is God, who also gave to us the earnest of the Spirit."

This immortal reconstruction of our body, and not the intermediate state, is that whereto God has destined us, and towards which his operations on us are tending. In the words before us Paul seems to allude to the workman's agency in fitting wood for building. By his energy and skill the rough stem of the tree is sawn, planed and polished, till it becomes fit for the temple or the palace. God has destined us for the conjoint life of body and soul. Indeed the intermediate state is not called " life " in Scripture, but " sleep." It is inactivity; and the essence of life and its enjoyment is activity.

The Holy Spirit was given as the proof of God's intention in this matter; as the witness both to the believer himself, and to the world. But this " earnest of the Spirit " may have two senses. (1) It may refer to the Holy Spirit's indwelling in all the saints. Without that, we should not be the sons of God, or able to address God as our Father in prayer. But this indwelling of the Spirit is a matter of faith to the saints now. To prove it we must point to Scripture. But this indwelling of the Holy Spirit, as the apostle informs us, is a pledge of resurrection. The Spirit

* The change of bodies is necessary, says Paul, to fit us for entry on " the kingdom of God." Therefore the kingdom of God does not begin till after the resurrection.

that dwells in our mortal bodies is the same that dwelt in Christ, the Spirit of immortal life. As then the Saviour rose from the dead through the power of the living God, whose Spirit abode in him, so shall we : Rom. viii, 11.

(2) But the pledge or " earnest of the Spirit " in its full and primary sense intends the gifts of the Spirit : the supernatural powers bestowed of old on believers in Jesus. They separated the saint vividly from the worldly, and were the visible seal of God, proving to the most prejudiced and unbelieving, the Deity dwelling within. They also silently foretold the noble destiny of such, as heirs of the coming kingdom. They were a pledge or partial performance by the Most High of his promises, bending him to their full accomplishment, which can only be in resurrection.

6. " Therefore we are always confident and assured that while at home in the body, we are from home* in regard of the Lord."

The internal operations of God's sanctifying Spirit, and his sensible gifts in them, sustained the courage of the saints against the alarms of the way. God's design must surely take effect at last. " Come then what may, we are bold. Whether we be spared till Christ comes, or life be taken from us ere then, our destiny is happiness." Some courage is founded on ignorance. The Christian's rest on knowledge. The more clear our appreciation of God's purposes of mercy towards his faithful servants, with the greater intrepidity may we face the dangers that beset us.

In the previous part of the chapter, the better alternative of the Christian, the being found alive at the Lord's coming, was proposed to our notice. Now the apostle treats of the other alternative—the dying or falling asleep before the Lord appears. This also, far from being an evil, is preferable, as is now to be declared, to life in the body. Such a view of our position may well sustain confidence. Either way the Christian is blest. The farmer would feel at ease

* $E\nu\delta\eta\mu\text{ουντεϛ.}$ $E\kappa\delta\eta\mu\text{ουμενα}$

with regard to his property who could say, when told of incendiaries near, " The news does not trouble me : if they do not come shortly, I shall have sold all my stock ; if they do, I am insured."

The verse now under consideration teaches us what becomes of the spirit of the saint at its departure. When death turns him out of the earthly tent he is brought into the presence of Christ. According to the figure of the text, he passes out of a foreign country where Christ is invisible, into another where the Saviour is beheld. For there are two regions ; one of sense, where the things temporary engage us, and the things eternal are unseen : and the other, that of the separate state, where the things unseen, and, above all, the Lord himself, burst upon us. The Jew might have his dwelling in Babylon. While there he could not behold his temple. He must travel to his father's land to gain a view of that glory of his nation.

To the believer of clear faith, this view does away with the terrors of death. Behind this scene· of the visible Jesus stands ready to manifest himself to them. Death, then, is an introduction to one whom he has long loved : and when we are journeying to those whom we love, the way is not irksome. This is the secret of the victorious deaths granted to many. May we so love the Lord, that what shall bring us home to him shall not be to us terrible !*

7. " For we walk by faith, not by sight."

This parenthesis is thrown in, by way of explaining to us how we are from home in reference to the Lord, while alive in the body. It would discomfort the saint greatly to be

---

* How this being ushered into the presence of Christ is to be reconciled with the equally clear doctrine that the saints are in Hades, and not in heaven, till the resurrection, I do not feel called on to discuss. The Scripture affirms both truths ; and both are to be received. They are reconcilable, whether we can see the way or no. The question hinges on the powers of perception possessed by separate spirits : a question on which we are ignorant.

given to understand that life was the period of Christ's total absence. How is he to be sustained without the Saviour's perpetual presence ? The Holy Spirit, therefore, defines in what sense the absence of the Lord from the present scene is to be taken.

He is present with *us* believers always. He is peculiarly present according to his promise, with the assembly of believers met in his name. He fills all things. But that is his presence with us, realized only by faith. But death brings *us* consciously, and as by a new sense, into *his presence.*

Faith is exchanged for sight. We cease to be exiles when once we have crossed the mountains of death.

We are away from Christ here, not as regards his knowledge of us, or his grace to sustain us, but in regard to our knowledge and sight of him. To him there is no darkness, where to us there is no light. The absence of the view of the Lord is the very characteristic of our dispensation. To Israel in the wilderness, and under Solomon, the visible abode of God among them was granted. But now, " Blessed are they that have not seen, and yet have believed." The return of Christ, exhibiting him once more as an object of sight, will close the present dispensation, and be the basis of one altogether different.

8. " But we are confident, and prefer rather to be from home as regards the body, and at home as regards the Lord."

Though our information concerning what lies beyond the visible scene of the bodily eye is derived only from the testimony of God, yet we hold it as certain as if our knowledge were obtained by the senses. The unbeliever trusts to his senses, and credits not God's simple word. We rest on that, believing it more trustworthy than the senses.

The state of the departed spirit is better in God's sight than that of the present life. " To be with Christ is far better." Life is only to be desired as the time of testimony for the Lord and of service to him, to be rewarded by Christ at his appearing. " If I live in the flesh, this is to me fruit of labour."*

But the state of the separate spirit is peace, and the absence of the trials of life. There the wicked have no more that they can do.

Thus there are three homes. 1. The present one, of the body. 2. That of the saintly spirit, at home with the Lord. The Lord is supposed to abide in his place, while we are introduced into his presence. This state continues till the Lord leaves the heaven and descends into the air, calling the living to his side, and at the same time reclothing the departed with their bodies. 3. This last state is the presence of Christ, which is especially to be the object of our desire. It is also the abiding one. " And so shall we be ever with the Lord."

" To be present with the Lord ! " How stinted, how meagre the information concerning that state ! God does not desire to fasten our eyes upon it. More by far is told us of the final state. But how unlike is such rigid frugality to the copiousness of false revelations upon this interesting topic ! This is indeed one of the proofs of a Divine Hand at work upon our Scriptures.

9. " Wherefore, we are also ambitious,† that whether at home or from home, we may be well-pleasing to him."‡

Paul had said before that the Christian preferred to be present with the Lord. But he adds, that in consideration of our appearing before Christ, a further motive actuated him. We wish to please him. It should not be translated, " we *labour*, that we may be *accepted* of him." We are accepted already : " *accepted in* the Beloved " : Eph. i, 6. But after being received by faith, and by it united to Christ, our conduct as saints and servants of Christ comes into question before him. Thenceforward we are to strive to please him.

---

* Τουτο μοι καρπος εργου.   † Φιλοτιμουμεθα   ‡ Ευαρεστοι.

The word used signifies "we are ambitious." That is, the hope of praise and glory from Christ is a motive to our actions. The love of glory is not cut off from the believer. It is sinful to seek glory from the world, and in the world's way. But it is perfectly legitimate and accepted before God, to desire and to seek glory from Christ in the way he has pointed out. Paul tells us of his ambition to preach the Gospel where Jesus' name had not been before heard of : Rom. xv, 20. (*Greek*.) The love of glory is not unbecoming the Christian. Crowns are to be won by service to God and his Christ. " Thou shalt have *glory* in the presence of them that sit at meat with thee." Jesus teaches us the way in which those who wish to be great may attain it in the coming kingdom : Matt. xx, 25–28.

The words " whether at home or from home " indicate the two states in which the disciples will be found at the Saviour's coming. Some will be among the living, some asleep. Those well pleasing to Christ will not be of the number found naked before him. Thus the dependence of shame or glory before Christ upon our life here, is once more brought into view.

10. " For we must all be manifested before the judgment-seat of the Christ, that each may receive the things done by means of the body, according to what he hath done, whether good or evil."

Behold more fully developed to us what the apostle intended by the being found naked ! It concerns the Saviour's investigation of our life. In the former portion, our glory or shame was referred to the time of putting on our immortal body. Here, another, but an accordant view, is given of it. The time of the award is to be the appearing of the Messiah, and his session on the judgment-seat. Then are the acts of our life to come before him.

All our actions, whether good or evil, are to be estimated. Saints are to be judged ; and it is supposed that some of their actions are evil. But they must be accounted for to Christ. When the separate spirit has been constituted a man again, by the restoration of his body, the question of his life in the body is fully gone into. It is then that some saints will be found naked : guilty of acts of deceit, uncleanness, covetousness, drunkenness, and other sins, from which some of the more amiable and decent of the worldly are free. Such will be ashamed before Christ. The parables which relate to the Saviour's judgment of the saint, discover that rebuke, exclusion from the kingdom, and disgrace, will as truly be features of that day of award, as praise, reception, and reward will be to others of the saints.

" *We* must *all* be manifested." Whether in the body or out of it, the two classes must both pass this seat of judgment. It is observable, that in judging the church, Jesus is said to sit on his judgment-seat,* while in judging the dead at the close of the thousand years, he is seated on his *throne.*

We must be " manifested." The investigation will not be with closed doors. Each will stand apart in his turn, and in open court give in his account. Our persons will be exhibited, our characters thoroughly disclosed.

We shall carry away the results. Our life with its series of actions is compared to a treasure long laid up under the Judge's care, and by him delivered to us, when the time of making over the deposit to us is come. For deeds of good, whether open or concealed from human eye, the recompense will be openly given by the Father. But what if the saint have been guilty, openly or in secret, of deeds of evil ? He shall carry away the recompense according to his deserts. " According to that he hath done "—Here is the principle of reward according to works.

11. " Knowing therefore the fear of the Lord, we persuade men, but are made manifest to God ; but I trust that we are made manifest in your consciences also."

* Βημα, Also Rom. xiv, 10.
† Φοβος.

By our translators rendering the word† in this case
" terror," it seems evident, that they supposed the apostle
to be referring to the ungodly, as though he had said—
" Knowing therefore the awfulness of the damnation of the
lost, we entreat men to escape it." But the apostle is
speaking of the judgment of saints alone.

It is a vindication of his sincerity in his ministry, as the
next verse proves. Having engrafted in his soul this
wholesome awe of the Lord's judgment he was kept steady
to his purpose, and to the service of Christ. Who could be
a hypocrite, that knows and believes this doctrine ? His
persuasion of men refers apparently to the arguments which
he used with his various opponents, to convince them of
his integrity. As though he said—" I am at the pains of
seeking to prove my sincerity and disinterestedness to *men*,
by arguments and appeals to circumstances. But before
God I need them not. He knows it, who searches out all my
ways." " And," he adds, " I trust that my uprightness is
apparent to you also, and that my appeals have carried
conviction to your consciences."

The apostle appears to say, that the belief and assertion
of this doctrine is a general guarantee for the uprightness
of him who holds and teaches it. He who trusts for his
security to his being elect of God, neglecting the equally
clear doctrines of accountability and consequent recompense, may fall into sin, either secretly or openly. But he
in whose soul this is unwoven as a first principle, cannot be
a hypocrite. The attempt to approve himself to God will
keep him blameless before man. Such an one must feel
how foolish it were to conceal sin from men, when to God
the secret is fully known, and when the very concealment
will be but the ground of more severe judgment when the
deeds of life, whether good or evil, are brought before the
tribunal of Christ. For as he has assured us, " there is
nothing covered, that shall not be revealed ; nor hid, that
shall not be known."

SELECTED WRITINGS

OF

ROBERT GOVETT, M.A.

EXPOSITIONS.

Romans.—The Righteousness of God. Cloth, gold lettered. 6s. 6d. net.

Galatians.—Moses or Christ? Cloth, gold lettered. 5s. net.

Ephesians.—What is the Church? Cloth, gold lettered. 4s. 6d. net.

Colossians.—Christ the Head. Cloth, gold lettered. 4s. 6d. net.

Philippians.—Fourth Kingdom and its City. Paper cover. 1s. 6d. net.

Thessalonians I. and II.—Presence of Christ. Paper cover. 1s. net.

Hebrews.—Christ Superior to Moses. Cloth, gold lettered. 7s. 6d. net.

I. John.—The Trinity, the Christ, and Antichrists. Cloth, gold lettered. 4s. net.

Revelation.—The Apocalypse Expounded by Holy Scripture. 630 pages. Crown 8vo. Cloth, gold lettered. 7s. 6d. net.

THE NEW JERUSALEM, OUR ETERNAL HOME. Cloth, gold lettered. 3s. 6d. net.

THE SERMON ON THE MOUNT EXPLAINED. Third Edition. Cloth, gold lettered. 3s. 6d. net.

ENTRANCE INTO THE KINGDOM: or, REWARD ACCORDING TO WORKS. Part I. Second Edition. Cloth, gold lettered. 4s. net.

Complete lists from—

A. J. TILNEY, 30, ALL SAINTS GREEN, NORWICH; or
CHAS. J. THYNNE, WHITEFRIARS ST., LONDON, E.C.4.

PRESENT-DAY PAMPHLETS

BY

D. M. PANTON, B.A.

The above ten Pamphlets, bound in one volume, cloth boards, with gold lettering, price 7/6 net. Post free, 8/-.

LONDON : CHAS. J. THYNNE.

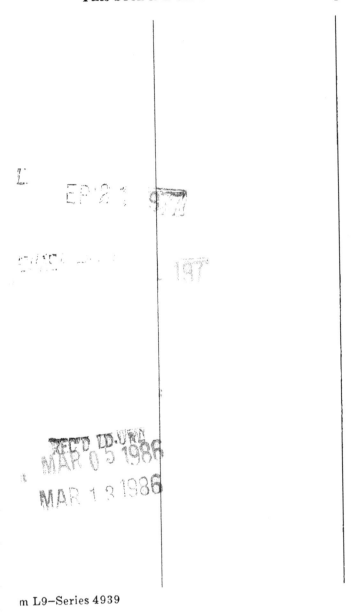

Made in the USA
Columbia, SC
15 March 2019